D1224352

AQUARIUM FISH

Originally published as *Poissons d'Aquarium* by Éditions Solar

This edition published by Barnes & Noble, Inc.,
by arrangement with Copyright S.A.R.L.

1999 Barnes & Noble Books

English translation by Ray Lurie
Editorial consultant, Jim Breheny
Electronic pagination and redesign by Carole Desnoes

ISBN 0-7607-0853-3

Printed and bound in Spain

99 00 01 02 03 M 9 8 7 6 5 4 3 2 1

Cayfosa

AQUARIUM FISH

Marc Ladonne

WITH

Marie-Paule Piednoir and Henri Grandcolas

PHOTOGRAPHS

Matthieu Prier

Contents

Practical Guide

The aquarium and its placement

The first thing you must think about is the aquarium itself. Keep in mind that aquariums should never be set up in direct sunlight. This will cause unwanted algae growth and elevated water temperatures at different times of the day. Choose a place that is away from drafts and direct sunlight. One of the nicest features of having an aquarium in the home is that it can bring life and activity to an otherwise dreary area. Next, you must remember that the larger the volume of water the aquarium holds, the easier it is to achieve and maintain an ecological balance. In order to select the proper aquarium, you need to reach a compromise between aesthetics and the conditions necessary to maintain this balance. Manufacturers of aquariums tend to lean toward the aesthetic side, making tanks that are longer and higher than they are wide. This practice cuts down on surface area, which is important for proper gas exchange. The greater the surface area, the more oxygen can get into the system. If you choose a tank with a large volume of water, yet proportionately little surface area, the need for good mechanical aeration and filtration systems becomes more important.

In general, after deciding what type of aquarium you would like to set up and then choosing an appropriate location, the next concern is usually financial. You should always purchase the largest aquarium you can afford that will be suitable for the location.

When filling your tank, in most cases it is not necessary to worry about the composition of the tap water. The chemistry of the water will change and evolve in the weeks after the tank is set up. This evolution is brought about by the choice of substrate, driftwood, and other ornamental pieces, the density of fish and other living organisms, and the amount and types of food that you feed. Add the substrate first, then place a bowl or saucer on it. Next, pour the water onto the saucer so as to not upset the gravel and stir up any fine particles. Fill the tank only two-thirds full, then add any rocks, plants, and other furnishings. This will prevent the tank from overflowing and allow the plants some support while you get an idea of how they will stand in the completed setup.

You can add commercial bacteria or bacteria from a filter that has been in a healthy tank. In either case, you want the bacteria to start a cycle of decomposition in the tank. Let the tank cycle for a week or so, and then start to add fish *slowly, a few at a time,* and allow the cycle to become firmly established.

Choose the fish in accordance with their water quality demands. Choose them by family and always buy groups of compatible fish. Do not just pick out single examples of different fish, and avoid disparities in size.

The water and its composition

Most aquarium hobbyists use tap water, the chemical characteristics of which can easily be treated, if needed, to meet the environmental demands of different fish. These demands correspond to the proper levels of pH and DH.

The pH or "potential of hydrogen"

This pH of water indicates the acidity or alkalinity of the water and is measured on a scale that ranges from 1 to 14. The water is acid if it is under 7; alkaline, or basic, if above 7; neutral, if 7. Most freshwater fish live in water with a pH of 6 to 8. This means that a fish that prefers to live in acid water (water with a pH lower than 7) will not live for a long time in an aquarium filled with alkaline water, and vice versa. For saltwater fish, the optimum pH is between 8 and 8.5.

The DH or "German degrees of hardness"
(Deutsche Härtegrad)

DH indicates the hardness of the water, that is, the quantity of mineral salts dissolved in the water. In nature, this measurement varies, obviously enough, as a result of the kinds of soils through which rainwater is filtered.

In order to breed the Hemichromis sp. *successfully, freshwater with a DH between 0 and 10 is needed.*

The two principal tests used to verify the water quality of an aquarium: the DH or "German degrees of hardness" (near right), and the pH or "potential of hydrogen" (far right).

The water is soft when the DH is between 0 and 10; moderately hard, from 10 to 20; hard, from 20 to 30; very hard, above 30. The DH, like the pH, can be measured with test kits sold in specialty shops.

Nitrogen

In fact, the most important considerations for the success of an aquarium are the nitrogen and ammonia cycles; next, the ammonium and nitrite cycles; and, last, the nitrate cycle. At each stage, specialized bacteria transform these toxic substances into nontoxic substances, which can then be metabolized by the plants. This is why it is essential for hobbyists to take care when choosing live plants for their aquarium and, above all, to wait several weeks before adding any fish. Such are the requirements of the nitrogen cycle.

Two simple rules

- To breed fish, the pH and DH levels should resemble those of the animal's native habitat as closely as possible.
- In order to prevent waste products from accumulating and to promote the nitrogen cycle, a portion of or approximately 20% of the water should be changed regularly. Such changes also replace trace elements necessary for living plants. In theory, one could measure the pH and DH levels of the water and fill the tank with water of the same composition, but normally, the water that has been siphoned off is simply replaced with tap water. Only a concern for the welfare of delicate fish and an interest in breeding push the aquarium hobbyist to replicate a particular kind of water.

The breeding of Haplochromis rostratus *requires a pH of 8.*

The lighting of the aquarium

Although the lighting, in and of itself, has little influence on the fish, it does play an important role in plant growth and in the health of certain marine invertebrates. A simple rule can be used to achieve suitable lighting for the volume of the aquarium: either 1 watt for every 3 qt (3 L) of water (dim lighting) or 1 watt for every 2 qt (2 L) of water (bright lighting). Standard fluorescent tubes meet these needs:

Length	**Strength**
18 in (45 cm)	15 W
24 in (60 cm)	18 W
30 in (75 cm)	25 W
36 in (90 cm)	30 W
48 in (120 cm)	36 W

These figures are rough guides and do not take into account either the depth of the water in the tank or the distance between the tubes and the water surface. For example, in a tank with a water depth of 20 in (50 cm), only 40% of the light generated reaches the bottom of the tank! Besides fluorescent tubes, there are also halogen lamps, mercury-vapor lamps, and so on, which are powerful, precise, and costly. They can be found in specialty shops, and your pet shop owner can advise you on what is best for your situation.

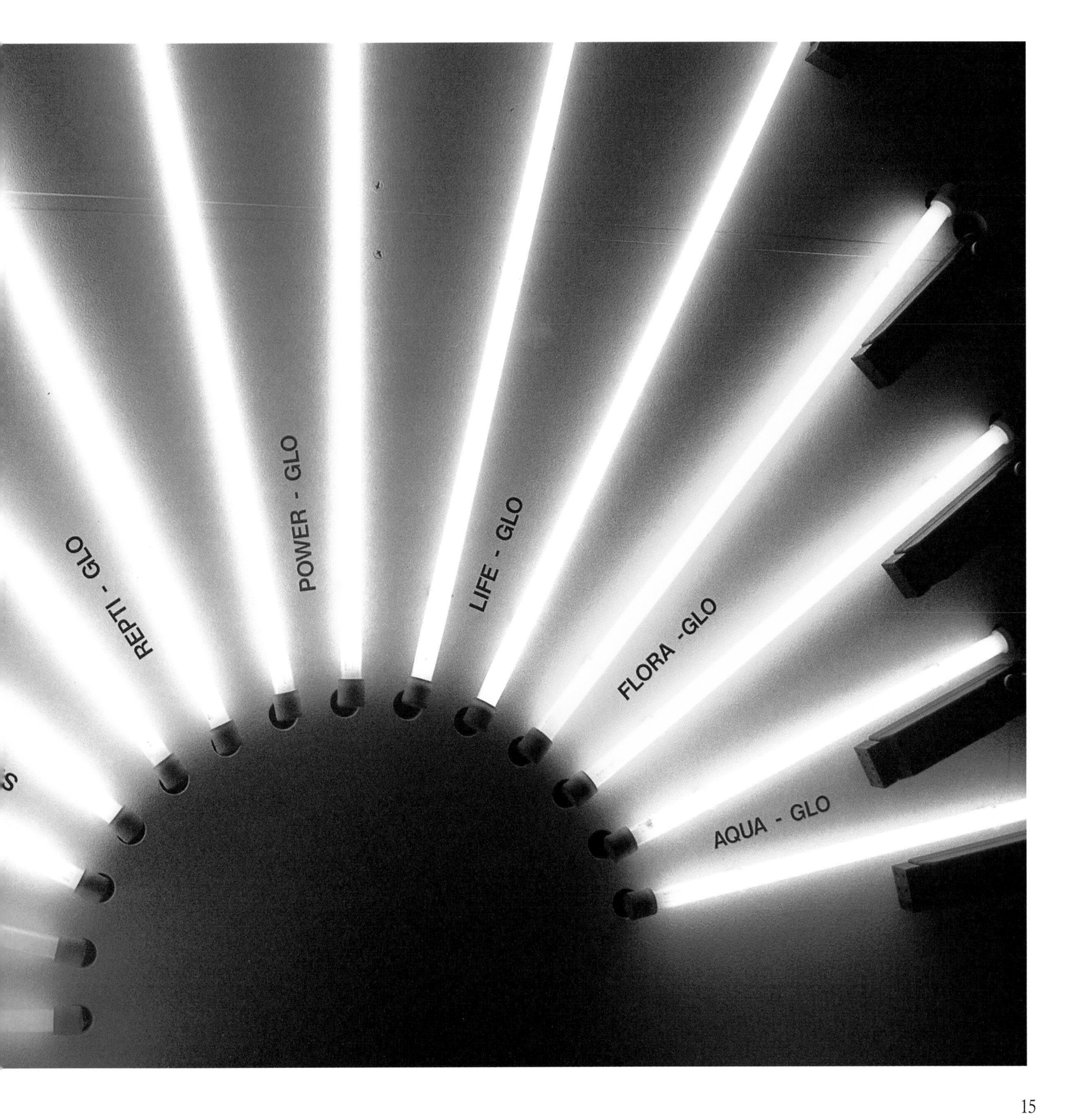
REPTI - GLO
POWER - GLO
LIFE - GLO
FLORA -GLO
AQUA - GLO

Filtration

Obviously, in nature there is no need for filtration because the aquatic system is able to decompose, recycle, and regenerate itself. In the aquarium, filters substitute for this natural capacity. We can distinguish between two types of filtration. First, mechanical filtration uses synthetic filter material along with some form of activated carbon. The synthetic material retains the waste particles suspended in the water, thereby keeping the water clean. The carbon traps gases and chemicals that can build up. The second type, biological filtration, allows the aquarium to purify itself by establishing bacterial growth as a source of natural decomposition, regeneration, and chemical balance.

Internal filters

The simplest type of internal filter is called an under-gravel filter and is comprised of a perforated, plastic sheet equipped with lift tubes that can be supplied with air by means of a vibrator pump or use a motorized powerhead to move the water. This is a prime example of biological filtration. Lying at the bottom of the aquarium, the filter plate is covered by a bed of gravel to a depth of at least 2 in (5 cm). While filtering the water, the gravel allows the growth of bacterial colonies.

A canister filtration system in the interior of an aquarium. This system is efficient but bulky and sharply reduces the usable volume of water reserved for the fish. Therefore, it is less desirable than other filtration systems in most circumstances.

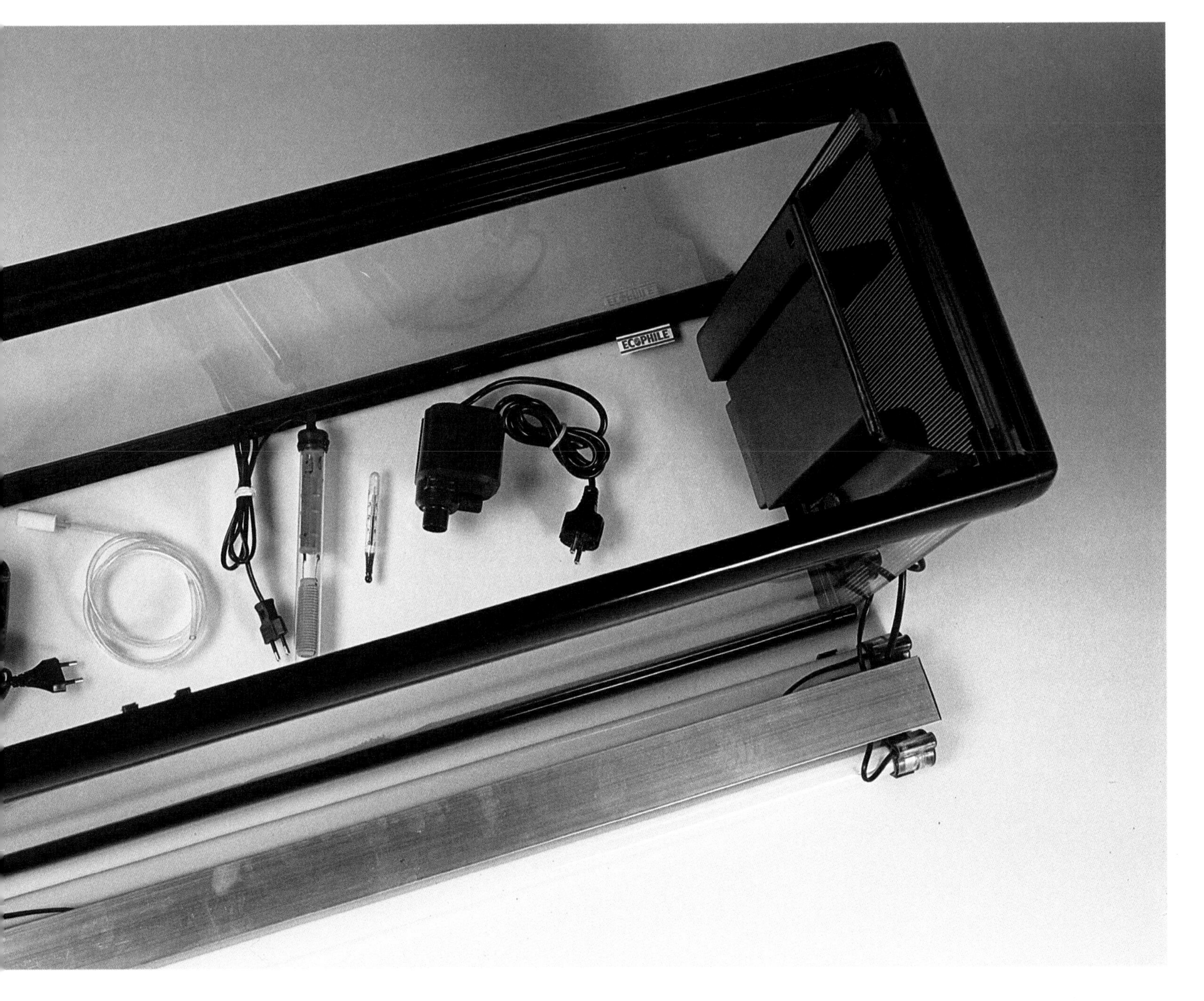

An external filter—not very attractive but very effective if you observe certain precautions while placing it for installation.

The advantages of an under-gravel filtration system are its low cost and relatively inconspicuous appearance. On the other hand, the gravel can become saturated with waste and require frequent cleaning. Most commonly, the filter plate is connected to a motorized powerhead, available in a great variety of sizes for moving the desired amount of water.

Internal canister filters

Internal canister filters are placed inside the aquarium and are run by a motor that draws the water in for filtration. Once filtered, the clean water is returned to the aquarium. Though these systems are easily maintained, they still suffer from an unwieldy size, which significantly reduces the usable area within the tank. External canister filters are more preferable. They are typically used with large aquariums, and although fairly costly and sizable, they provide a large filtration capacity and are easy to maintain.

External filters

With an external filter, the water is siphoned from the aquarium into the tank of the filter, which is filled with mechanical and biological filter materials, and is returned to the aquarium after passing through the filter. Despite the tubing, this system is easy to conceal and offers a high filtration capacity. Some external filters hang on the back of the aquarium while others are contained in canisters. These canister systems (like the one pictured above) tend to be more expensive and can present a risk of "siphonage" in cases where the filter is improperly installed or there is a power failure. In order to avoid such risk, it is best to place the filter at a position *higher* than the aquarium. Even if this is neither practical nor attractive, it is better in case of an accident, and will prevent the tank from emptying itself out onto the carpet!

The under-gravel filter, an example of a biological filtration system, is simple and inexpensive. Nonetheless, the filtration capacity of the gravel is limited.

Aquarium plants

Before all the elaborate filtration systems aquarists have at their disposal today, living plants were an important part of the aquarium ecosystem. Besides adding to the beauty of the aquarium, they produced the oxygen needed by the aquatic inhabitants and metabolized the nitrates, thereby contributing to the whole biological equilibrium of the aquarium. But plants are living organisms that must be maintained within a specific group of parameters, and therefore come with their own set of problems and needs. Today, because of advances in mechanical systems, living plants are not vital to the aquarium. Many people choose to use plastic aquarium plants instead. These plastic substitutes provide the tank inhabitants with most of the benefits of live plants and relieve the hobbyist's burden of trying to manage the needs of a whole other group of organisms. Purists would argue, however, that keeping and maintaining living aquarium plants is part of the experience. The following section is for those aquarists who wish to keep live plants in the aquarium.

Substrate

Aquarium gravel is not always the best substrate in which to grow aquarium plants. For this reason, many aquarists keep live plants in their own individual pots or planting containers. In this way, a special planting substrate or rooting material can provide the plants with the nutrients they need for healthy growth. In addition to these special substrates, numerous fertilizers can be purchased in your aquarium shop. They can be in liquid or solid form and can be used with success if the directions are followed.

Examples of plants for an Amazonian aquarium.

Water

The majority of aquarium plants adapt to water having a mean pH of between 6.5 and 7.5, inclusive, and a DH, or degrees of hardness, of around 20. Finally, you should avoid direct sunlight, which is difficult to regulate, and stick to the recommended period of twelve hours of light per day.

It is essential to note that plants that have a stem and roots must be planted so that the stem is in the water and not buried in the sand; otherwise, you risk a rapid decline in the plant's health.

What is the role of carbon dioxide gas in the growth of plants? The supply of additional CO_2 beyond that produced by the fish alone helps stimulate the root system. It also serves as a gentle way of lowering the pH. There are several commercial systems available to ensure this supply. The most elementary is by means of a simple aerosol can; the most complex consists of a feedback device that regulates the output of CO_2 in accordance with the desired pH level. If properly controlled, carbon dioxide gas prevents the growth of undesirable algae.

Plants to decorate the aquarium

In general, three sizes of plants are used: dwarf, medium, and large.

Among the dwarf plants, the most commonly used are the following:

• Dwarf *Cryptocoryne* plants, whose numerous varieties allow the choice of an infinite number of shapes and colors.

• Dwarf *Anubias,* which are semi-aquatic

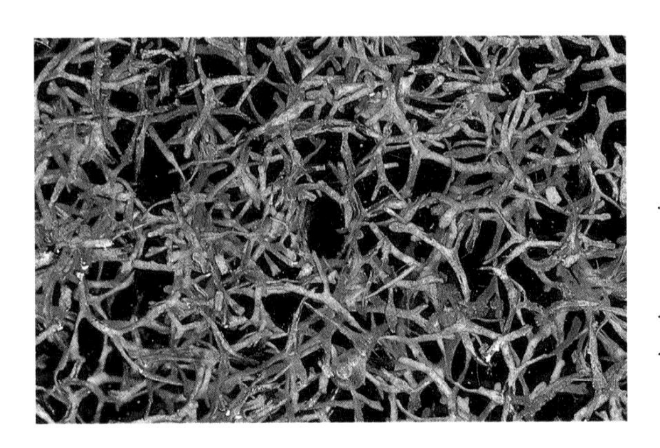

Left: This plant, Riccia, *commonly known as crystalwort, floats on the surface of the water. It is very useful for spawning and for filtering the light.*

Below: A selection of several plants frequently grown in the aquarium from the genera Echinodorus, Anubias, Microsorium, *and others.*

plants whose sturdy leaves adapt very well to immersion.

• *Lilaeopsis,* or aquarium grass, with small leaves that are an attractive dark or silvery green, depending on the variety.

Among the medium-sized plants, the most popular is still the *Cabomba,* which should be planted in conjunction with the *Hygrophila* and which includes numerous rapidly growing varieties. You may also wish to grow several varieties of *Echinodorus,* but these must be planted separately.

Finally, for the tall plants, there are the *Vallisneria* and the taller species of *Cryptocoryne* and *Echinodorus.* Bulb plants, such as *Aponogeton,* bring an inventive touch to the decoration because of their peculiar shapes. These plants, however, should be attempted only by the experienced aquarium enthusiast, because they are very sensitive to water quality and it is essential to respect their dormant periods in order to build up the strength of the bulb.

General rules

It should be noted that plants of a single species should always be planted in homogeneous groups.

Plants without roots, such as Javanese Moss (or *Riccia,* which is more difficult to obtain and lives on the surface), are also available. Although they are very useful for spawning and allow diffuse light to penetrate the water, they have the disadvantage of being extremely invasive.

Food

In nature, the principal activity of fish is their search for food, which leads them to expend a great deal of energy, especially if we consider the volume and space in which they swim. In nature, food—whether from animals or plants—never causes pollution problems. The case is entirely different in an aquarium, and the problems encountered are associated with the confined space and the absence of natural food, except for plants that are nibbled by certain omnivorous fish. Since the hobbyist provides them with their daily ration of food—and often with much more than this—we must consider how little energy is actually expended by the fish in feeding themselves. The result is that in a poorly filtered aquarium, all the uneaten food brings about a disastrously high level of pollution, putting the biological equilibrium of the whole tank into serious question.

It is therefore a good idea to feed the fish often but only a little at a time, and to vary their food as much as possible. Flake foods, granular foods, and tablets, not to mention live and frozen food from a reliable source, can be alternated as part of the feeding regime. It is better to buy packages of frozen food from stores serving the needs of fish hobbyists than to risk feeding with live catch from dubious or even unhealthy ponds, which could introduce parasites or diseases.

No food should be given in excessive quantities. Uneaten food results in a serious pollution problem, fouling the tank. In the case of flake and other dry food, only small amounts that can be consumed in five minutes or less should be fed. It is much better to feed smaller amounts more frequently than do one or two large feedings a day.

A well-nourished fish is one whose natural color and patterns are vibrant, intense, and brilliantly highlighted. A healthy fish is always ready to eat. But remember, be conservative in your feeding habits. Overfeeding is the most common cause of tanks becoming polluted and a definite contributing factor to fish mortality.

Below, left: Fish sharing a food tablet.

Right: Live insect larvae are a treat for most fish.

Diseases

To maintain healthy fish, you should always follow the time-tested proverb, "An ounce of prevention is worth a pound of cure." It is worth repeating that you should carefully choose the fish you want to have in your tank. First, you must consider the behavior of the species. Once you decide on the proper species, it is extremely important to start with healthy individuals. You should only buy fish from established pet shops with good reputations. The shop should be clean, the animals well cared for, and the owner and staff knowledgeable and willing to help and advise you. You should avoid any specimen showing any of the following signs: an emaciated appearance or sunken belly, spots or ulcers, cloudy eyes, trembling, clamped fins, halting swimming, and those gasping for air at the surface of the display tanks.

When you make your selection and take the fish home, it is advisable to keep the new acquisition in a small holding tank for a week or two to make sure it is healthy and will not introduce any disease to the fish already in your tank. Float the fish in the plastic bag in the small tank for at least twenty minutes. This will allow the water in the bag to reach the same temperature as the water in the tank. Next, you can make a small hole in the bag and gradually mix some of the water from the aquarium with the water that is in the bag. After this, the contents of the bag (including the fish) can be released. Keep the new fish there for a week to ten days. If any health problems arise, they can be treated and resolved before the fish goes into your established aquarium.

Despite all precautions, you will at one time or another experience some health problems and fish mortality in your tank. Some reasons might indicate:

- Fouled water with waste buildup in the aquarium. Ammonia, if not processed by bacteria, turns into nitrites, then nitrates. Regular partial water changes on a monthly basis help to reduce accumulated waste products.
- Parasites that can cause a variety of diseases in aquarium fish. Most of these parasites and the diseases they cause can be treated by a wide variety of medications on the market. Consult your aquarium shopkeeper with an accurate description of the symptoms so that you can be advised on the proper course of treatment.

Above, left: The small white spots characteristic of the Ichthyophthirius *parasite.*

Below, left: An ulcer on the body of a fish.

Above: Two healthy fish, showing no sign of an emaciated appearance, a sunken belly, spots, or ulcers. They have clear eyes, their fins are not attached, and they are swimming without any halting motions.

Aquatic environment

The large areas from which freshwater fish originate have different characteristics, which are useful to know in order to promote fish life in the aquarium. These areas may be divided into four zones.

Amazonian zone

This zone provides a home for the principal families of exotic fish: Characins, cichlids, and catfish are the largest of these families. The Amazonian waters, which are often dark, are fresh and have a low mineral content. Enormous floods constantly alter the levels and even the course of the rivers in this zone.

Central American zone

In the Central American zone lives the large family of Poeciliidae, from which come the most popular fish: guppies, platys, and swordtails. Several cichlids and characins also live in these alkaline and mineral-rich waters. Today, a number of tropical countries have introduced these fish into their rivers, where they thrive despite the water being noticeably different.

The Amazonian environment is home to characins, cichlids, and catfish, among others.

The African zone

It is mostly in the alkaline and moderately hard waters of Lake Tanganyika and Lake Malawi that the most beautiful cichlids in the world have evolved. The river fish from the softer and more acid waters of the west of Africa are also quite beautiful.

The Asian zone

The generally acid and soft waters of the Asian zone welcome the large family of cyprinids, which includes the goldfish, and the family of labyrinthfish, such as the bettas and the gouramis.

The Asian environment hosts cyprinids, such as the goldfish, and labyrinthfish, such as the bettas and the gouramis (pictured below).

Freshwater Fish

Cyprinidae

The cyprinidae are found on nearly every continent, where they live for the most part in freshwater. With more than 1,400 species, cyprinids are generally tranquil, hardy, and easy to care for. Their jaws, which are toothless, are instead placed on their pharyngeal bones.

Carassius auratus

GOLDFISH

- ➤ *Originally from China; later, from Japan; today, found in all fish-breeding areas*
- ➤ *6 to 7 ³⁄₄ in (15 to 20 cm)*
- ➤ *Cold and temperate waters*

Calm and peaceful

Nicknamed both "Chinese fish" and "Japanese fish," depending on their origin, goldfish today exhibit a large variety of shapes and colors. Ranging from white to black, with yellow, red, and blue as well, their markings display numerous different shades. Depending on the species, their shape is just as varied: oversized fins, an egg-shaped abdomen, and wartlike growths on the head. The hardy varieties thrive splendidly in outside pools, whereas varieties that have undergone excessive genetic modifications must spend at least the cold season indoors. They grow rapidly as long as they are adequately fed. As a result, the aquarium must be thoroughly filtered; a simple bowl is not adequate.

***Far left:* The common Goldfish.**

***Top:* The Shubunkin.**

***Below:* Calico Fantails.**

Near and far right: Red-and-White Ryukin.

Inset: A variant with distinctly redder coloration.

The Black Moor, a stunning variety.

Rasbora heteromorpha

Red Rasbora

➤ *Thailand, Malaysia* ➤ *2 in (5 cm)* ➤ *72° to 77°F (22° to 25°C)*
Pleasant

This attractive little fish, below—of an iridescent pink ending in a black triangle—is relatively hardy despite its small size. Blessed with an extraordinarily calm disposition, it has no difficulty living alongside all kinds of other species, even the Characidae. To show off all its colors, it is best kept in a school. It eats both live and dehydrated food. A tank with lush vegetation is necessary for it to feel comfortable. When softly lit, such a setting resembles its native environment.

Labeo bicolor

RED-TAILED SHARK

➤ *Thailand* ➤ *4 2/3 in (12 cm)* ➤ *73° to 81°F (23° to 27°C)*
Territorial, becomes aggressive as it ages

Strongly resembling the Rainbow Shark, this fish has a sharklike shape. The blood-red color of its tail alerts the other denizens of the aquarium to the predatory tendencies of this large omnivore. Even if it sometimes lurks during the day in the natural hiding places provided by the vegetation, it does not hesitate to show its intolerance toward its tankmates. This powerful swimmer ruthlessly hunts down the weakest fish. Some aquarium enthusiasts have noticed that by lowering the temperature of the water to 70°F (21°C), they can reduce the number of these violent incidents. This is an effective way of bringing peace to the sharks but is detrimental to the other residents of the aquarium, which may severely dislike this cooler temperature. The Red-tailed Shark is a voracious feeder and swallows everything. Reproduction in captivity is difficult and, in specialized breeding farms, is successful only with the use of hormone injections.

The velvety black color of the Labeo bicolor *appears when the fish is in good health.*

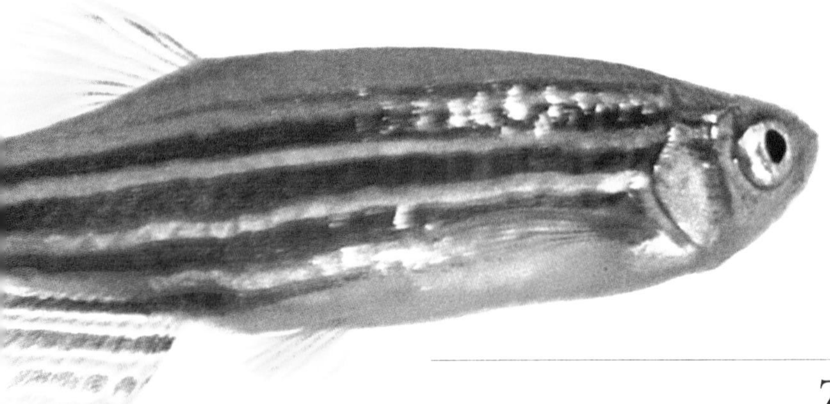

Brachydanio rerio

Zebra, Zebra Danio

➤ *India* ➤ *1 1/2 to 2 in (4 to 5 cm)* ➤ *64° to 75°F (18° to 24°C)*
Very peaceful but lively, with spirit

This fish, marked with five steel blue bands, delights the viewer as it swims about in its school. In a community tank, its urbanity makes it a peaceful companion for all the other small fish, except for those that require a calmer environment. It can be a fin nipper if kept with fish with long, flowing fins, such as bettas. Not finicky about the composition of the water, it also tolerates considerable differences in temperature–68°F (20°C) in extreme cases. We do not, though, advise you to test this in your aquarium! Nonetheless, if they need to breed, it is better that spawning take place in water between 75° and 79°F (24° and 26°C). In a small container of tap water, you should release two or three males and one female in order to ensure that all the eggs are fertilized. After spawning, remove all the partners in order to prevent them from eating the eggs.

The veil-finned form of the Zebra Danio. Steel-blue bands adorn the whole length of its body.

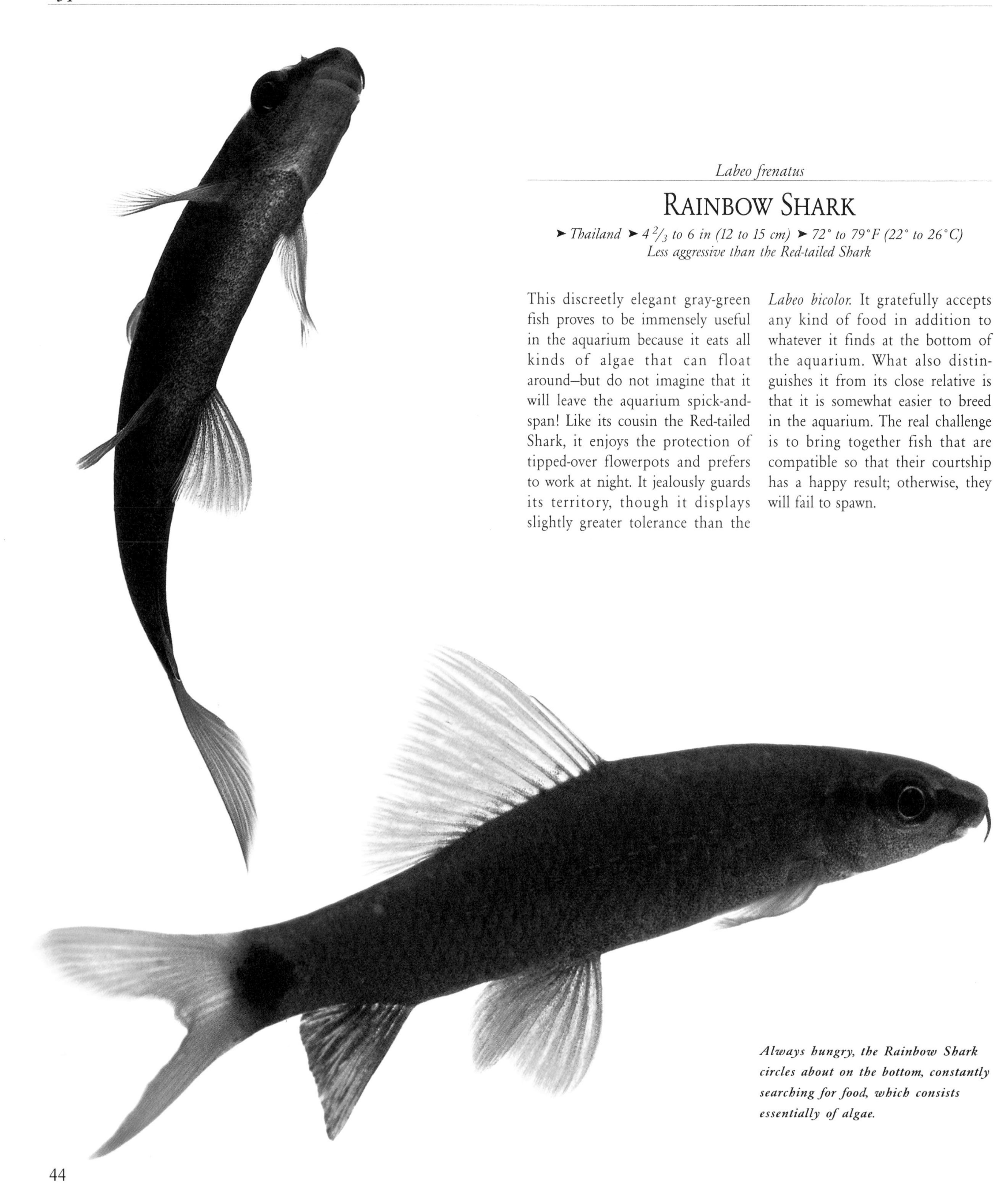

Labeo frenatus

RAINBOW SHARK

➤ *Thailand* ➤ *4 2/3 to 6 in (12 to 15 cm)* ➤ *72° to 79°F (22° to 26°C)*
Less aggressive than the Red-tailed Shark

This discreetly elegant gray-green fish proves to be immensely useful in the aquarium because it eats all kinds of algae that can float around–but do not imagine that it will leave the aquarium spick-and-span! Like its cousin the Red-tailed Shark, it enjoys the protection of tipped-over flowerpots and prefers to work at night. It jealously guards its territory, though it displays slightly greater tolerance than the *Labeo bicolor.* It gratefully accepts any kind of food in addition to whatever it finds at the bottom of the aquarium. What also distinguishes it from its close relative is that it is somewhat easier to breed in the aquarium. The real challenge is to bring together fish that are compatible so that their courtship has a happy result; otherwise, they will fail to spawn.

Always hungry, the Rainbow Shark circles about on the bottom, constantly searching for food, which consists essentially of algae.

Tanichthys albonubes, *a favorite variety with beginners.*

Tanichthys albonubes

WHITE CLOUD MOUNTAIN FISH

➤ *China* ➤ *1 1/2 in (4 cm)* ➤ *Tolerates temperatures from 41° to 77°F (5° to 25°C)*
Sociable

This fish has simple needs, which makes it a good fish for beginners. The water temperature does not make much difference to it. It can adapt to water temperatures between 41° and 77°F (5° and 25°C), but in order for the fish to spawn, the water needs to be at least 72°F (22°C). The composition of the water is also unimportant. In addition, the fish is omnivorous: It accepts everything from flake food to small live foods. You should place some plants here and there where the young can retreat for several days in complete tranquillity after birth, although as long as they are adequately fed, the parents do not usually tend to eat their young.

Epalzeorhynchus kallopterus

Flying Fox

➤ *Sumatra, Borneo* ➤ *4 to 6 in (10 to 15 cm)* ➤ *72° to 79°F (22° to 26°C)*
Peaceful with other species, aggressive toward its own kind

The perfectly tapered body of the Flying Fox makes it an excellent swimmer. In addition to observing the dark stripe that runs the whole length of its body, notice the unusual position of its mouth. It is this that enables the fish to scrape clean the walls of the aquarium and all the various ornamental aquarium fixtures. This omnivorous creature harvests all the organic matter that is floating on the bottom of the aquarium. It acts very aggressively toward members of its own species. It may intimidate members of other species, but does not harm them at all. In captivity, its reproduction is rarely witnessed.

Epalzeorhynchus siamensis

Siamese Flying Fox

➤ *Malaysia, Thailand* ➤ *4 to 6 in (10 to 15 cm)* ➤ *72° to 79°F (22° to 26°C)*
Aggressive toward its own kind

A cousin of the Flying Fox, this fish is easily distinguished by its lighter tint and the black line that runs from the gill cover to the tail fin. It, too, is a hardy and solitary cleaning fish whose reproduction is rarely seen in the aquarium.

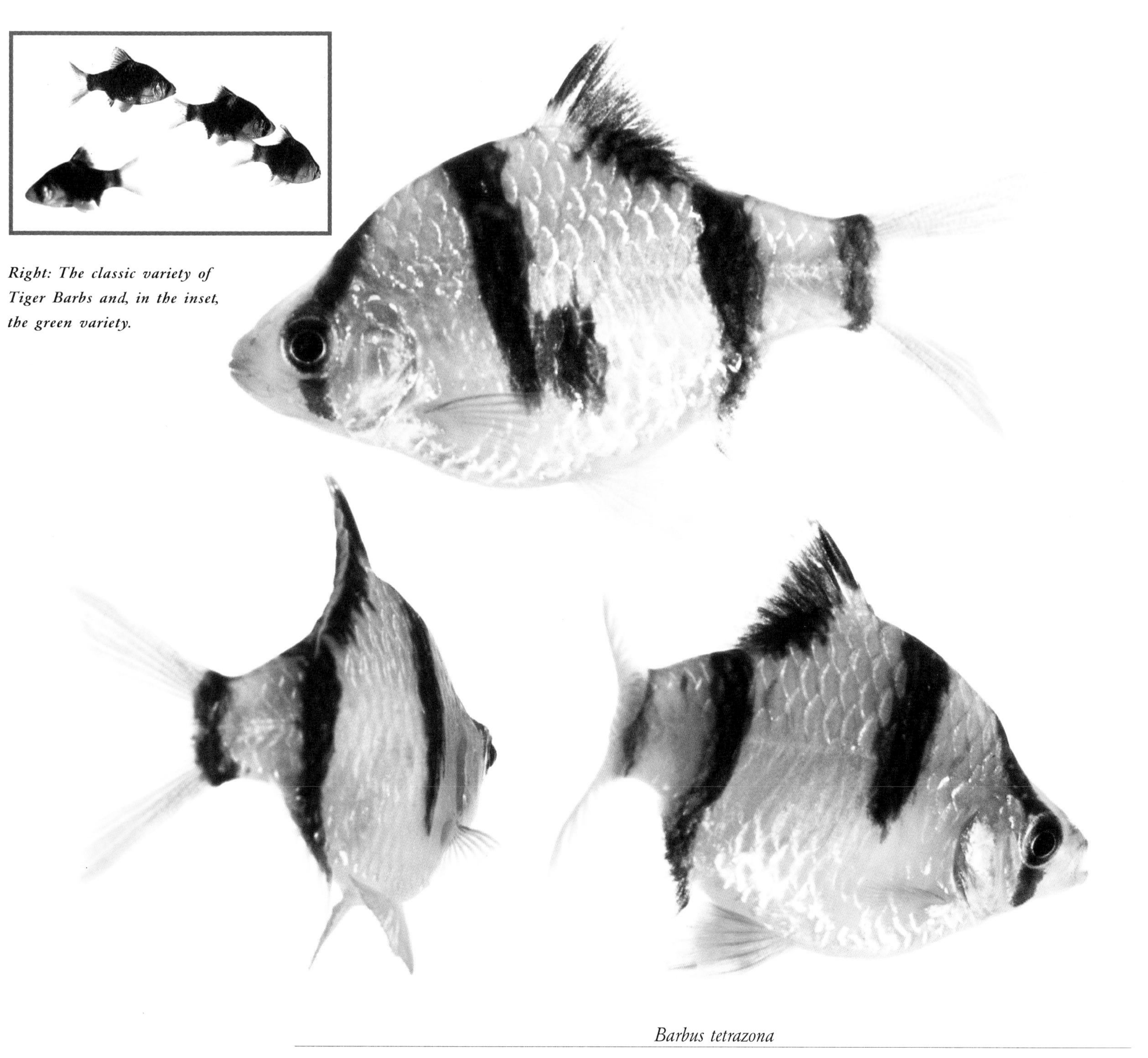

Right: The classic variety of Tiger Barbs and, in the inset, the green variety.

Barbus tetrazona

Tiger Barb

➤ *Sumatra, Borneo, perhaps Thailand* ➤ *2 1/3 to 3 in (6 to 8 cm)* ➤ *68° to 79°F (20° to 26°C)*
Playful

The Tiger Barb is one of the most popular aquarium fish. Whatever the principal color of its body, whether green or (more commonly) orangish-yellow, it is marked with four black stripes that cut vertically across its body. A closely related variety shows the beginning of a fifth stripe underneath the dorsal fin. The body of the female appears fuller, and its markings are less striking. Gregarious and active like all the other barbs, they are best kept in groups where their schooling behavior is easily observed. The Tiger Barb languishes in the company of slow swimmers and continually nips at their fins. It can tolerate freshwater of crystalline purity, even with large differences in temperature, from 68° to 79°F (20° to 26°C).

Barbus conchonius

Rosy Barb

➤ *Northern India*
➤ *2 1/3 to 3 in (6 to 8 cm)*
➤ *64° to 77°F (18° to 25°C)*
Sociable, but (as with all barbs) should not be placed in the same tank as veil-finned fish

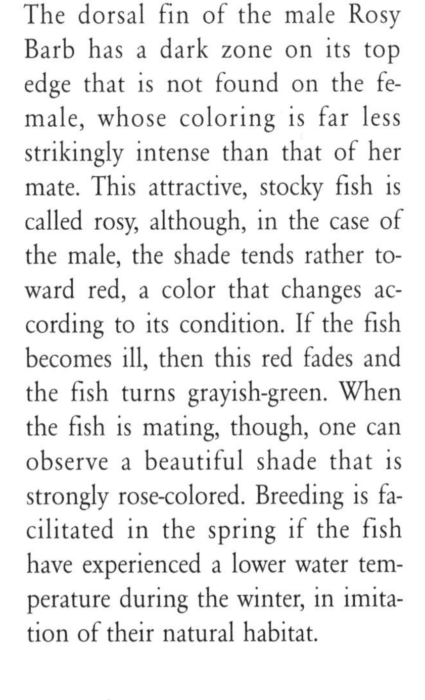

The dorsal fin of the male Rosy Barb has a dark zone on its top edge that is not found on the female, whose coloring is far less strikingly intense than that of her mate. This attractive, stocky fish is called rosy, although, in the case of the male, the shade tends rather toward red, a color that changes according to its condition. If the fish becomes ill, then this red fades and the fish turns grayish-green. When the fish is mating, though, one can observe a beautiful shade that is strongly rose-colored. Breeding is facilitated in the spring if the fish have experienced a lower water temperature during the winter, in imitation of their natural habitat.

Barbus schuberti

Brocaded Barb, Schuberti Barb

➤ *Southern Asia* ➤ *2 1/3 in (6 cm)* ➤ *68° to 75°F (20° to 24°C)*
Sociable

This attractive little fish makes a very nice addition to the tank. The golden yellow coat of this sprightly fish shows up well against the green background of the vegetation as it constantly darts about. When mating, its belly, normally pale yellow, turns as red as its fins. The Schuberti Barb is omnivorous, and it loves sun-drenched water. To keep it comfortable, it is a good idea not to let the temperature drop below 68°F (20°C).

Barbus titteya

Cherry Barb

➤ *Sri Lanka*
➤ *2 in (5 cm)*
➤ *73° to 79°F (23° to 26°C)*
Sociable

The handsomely tapered body of the male Cherry Barb is bronze red, marked along its length by a plain brown stripe. The fins of the male are red and brilliant; those of the female are rather yellowish and the color is generally duller. Like all barbs, it prefers to live as part of a school in a large aquarium. Its eggs adhere to the dense vegetation during spawning.

The Ember Barb likes to live in an aquarium well furnished with plants.

Barbus fasciatus

Banded Barb, Ember Barb

➤ *Malaysia* ➤ *2 $^{3}/_{4}$ in (7 cm)* ➤ *68° to 79°F (20° to 26°C)*
Peaceful

This very active fish prefers living in a school in a large aquarium that is rich in vegetation, where its liveliness and vivid colors are shown off to its advantage. Even if the males become combative during the mating season, their battles rarely cause harm. This species breeds as easily as other barbs, and you must exercise the same precautions with the parents, who enjoy consuming their offspring.

Cobitidae

The Cobitidae are found throughout the Old World, especially in Asia and in Europe, but also with several species in Africa. They are shy, omnivorous, and generally nocturnal fish. They have barbels and particularly unusual markings.

Botia macracantha

Clown Loach

➤ *Indonesia* ➤ *6 to 11 $^2/_3$ in (15 to 30 cm)* ➤ *77° to 82°F (25° to 28°C)*
Friendly

The Clown Loach is among those rare species that never breed in aquariums. However, in Indonesia, from where it is imported, it is a prolific breeder. This fish has many advantages. Brightly colored, it is very handsome and is, in fact, one of the most attractive representatives of its family; it is useful in the tank, since it eats snails; and it is completely nonaggressive. Its reputation for intelligence is thought to match the brightness of its exterior. This fish profits from sharing its territory with others of its species; alone, it is often unable to adapt. After purchasing this fish, you must be extremely vigilant because the Clown Loach is sensitive to the *Ichthyophthirius* parasite, which causes white-spot disease (ich). In the beginning, be especially careful about its food. Well nourished with *Tubifex* worms (whether frozen or alive), it soon grows to a respectable size, around 8 in (20 cm) in a large aquarium, and will swim happily all day long for up to ten years.

Acanthophthalmus kuhlii

Coolie Loach, Striped Loach, Leopard Eel, Prickly Eye

➤ *Southeast Asia* ➤ *Male: 3 in (7.5 cm); female: 4 to 4 2/3 in (10 to 12 cm)* ➤ *75° to 79°F (24° to 26°C)*
Nocturnal

The Coolie Loach knows how to make itself useful–it constantly digs around in the sand and swallows whatever debris is lying about. Accommodating, hardy, and attractive, it lives in groups whose members swarm together like a nest of vipers. Relaxing in the various nooks and crannies where it hides, it drives its owners to despair, since they are forced to wait until nightfall in order to catch even the smallest glimpse of their charge, for Coolie Loaches do not go out during the day. And although this Asian fish is hardy, its skin is delicate. You should avoid placing it in a tank with gravel on the bottom. While it is burrowing, the sharp edges of the gravel can cause skin abrasions which could lead to infection. A bed of very fine sand forms an ideal surface on which it can furrow about without running any risk of injury.

Botia striata

ZEBRA LOACH

➤ *Java, Thailand, India* ➤ *2 1/3 to 4 in (6 to 10 cm)* ➤ *77°F (25°C)*
Peaceful

In addition to enjoying the beauty of its markings, this relatively nonaggressive fish is exceptionally useful: It destroys unwanted snails that can end up invading the aquarium with the introduction of live plants. It is not as unruly as its cousin the Clown Loach, although both of these species show considerable tolerance and live easily in the same tank with other fish. Happily living hidden amid the plants and roots, nocturnal in habit, it escapes the notice of its owners, who, with good reason, would wish to see it more often.

Characidae

The majority of small fish that are found in domestic aquariums are from this large family. A large number of them are originally from South America (especially from the Amazon basin) or from Africa. Although characins prefer freshwater with either a neutral pH or a slight acidity, they can also acclimate themselves to harder water. The difficulty of breeding them in the aquarium as well as their unspectacular appearance explain why collectors are generally uninterested in raising them.

Pristella maxillaris

PRISTELLA, X-RAY FISH

➤ *Amazon* ➤ *2 in (5 cm)* ➤ *75° to 82°F (24° to 28°C)*
Peaceful

This fish prefers acid water. Clear and yellow-green over the largest part of its body, it has a black mark on its dorsal, anal, and pelvic fins. Living in a group agrees with it, and it shows great tolerance for other fish. It makes its home in freshwater with dappled light, filtered through greenery. As for food, it enjoys *Tubifex* worms and daphnia, along with flake food. To its credit, the Pristella is a very good breeder, so long as you find a pair that are compatible.

Hyphessobrycon herbertaxelrodi

Black Neon Tetra

➤ *Amazon*
➤ *1 to 1 1/2 in (3 to 4 cm)*
➤ *73° to 79°F (23° to 26°C)*
Calm

Accustomed to living in a group, this very attractive tetra does not present any special difficulty. Hardy and peaceful, it is nonetheless sensitive to the *Ichthyophthirius* parasite. Good oxygenation of the water is needed to ensure its well-being. As for its food, it can eat small live insects and their larvae as well as flake food.

Thayeria boehlkei

Penguin Fish

➤ *Amazon* ➤ *2 1/3 to 3 in (6 to 8 cm)* ➤ *72° to 81°F (22° to 27°C)*
Playful

The Penguin Fish, which has a black stripe running its entire length, from the gill cover to the end of the caudal fin, is one of the most sociable of all fish. Although it is a good companion for fish its own size, it cannot help teasing smaller fish, shamelessly nibbling at their fins. Since this fish is somewhat particular about the quality of its water, it is important that the water be clear of decomposing organic matter: Above all, this fish dislikes nitrites. Regular water changes will help keep it free from disease.

Hemigrammus erythrozonus

Glowlight Tetra

➤ *Guiana* ➤ *$1\frac{1}{2}$ to 2 in (4 to 5 cm)*
➤ *73° to 81°F (23° to 27°C)*
Gregarious

The delicate copper-colored reflections that saturate its skin give this attractive neon its pink tint. Slender and peaceful, it is the ideal companion in an aquarium filled with other small fish. Even though it swallows flake food without complaint, it nonetheless shows a clear preference for small worms. All that is needed to obtain the proper conditions for breeding is to raise the water to a temperature between 79° and 82°F (26° and 28°C), add a few additional plants to the surrounding vegetation, and dim the lights.

Gasteropelecus sternicla

Silver Hatchetfish

➤ *Amazon, Guiana* ➤ *$2\frac{1}{2}$ in (6.5 cm)* ➤ *75° to 82°F (24° to 28°C)*
Gregarious and sociable

Very abundant in the wild where it is collected, the hatchetfish is rarely bred in captivity. The Silver Hatchetfish, at $2\frac{1}{2}$ in (6.5 cm) in length, is slightly larger than the Marbled Hatchetfish, which rarely exceeds $1\frac{1}{2}$ in (4 cm). With a delicate complexion that is very susceptible to white-spot disease (ich), caused by the *Ichthyophthirius* parasite, the hatchetfish prefers to swim about in acid water. Sociable and peaceful, but not without spirit, the hatchetfish dreads nothing so much as rowdy neighbors. Its distinguishing characteristic is its mouth, which is situated at the apex of the triangle formed by its body and oriented toward the surface of the water, where the fish is nourished by trapping all kinds of small prey that come nearby. As a result, it cannot eat food from the bottom of the aquarium, nor even from the middle. If, however, you throw some insects or flies on the surface of the water, then the hatchetfish will jump for joy. Note, too, that its natural exuberance, paired with a genuine ability to fly out of the water, makes it necessary to place a cover on the aquarium.

As with all the other hatchetfish, we can observe great pectoral development on the* Carnegiella strigata, *or Marbled Hatchetfish.

Hyphessobrycon rosaceus

Rosy Tetra

➤ *South America*
➤ *$1^1/_2$ to 2 in (4 to 5 cm)*
➤ *75° to 82°F (24° to 28°C)*
Calm

This very sturdy and gregarious fish flourishes only when living in a group. Left alone or nearly alone, it is somewhat listless, its life span is shorter, and most of all, it fails to achieve the same intense coloration as when it lives in a school. This hardy fish can tolerate a variety of conditions but prefers soft, slightly acid water.

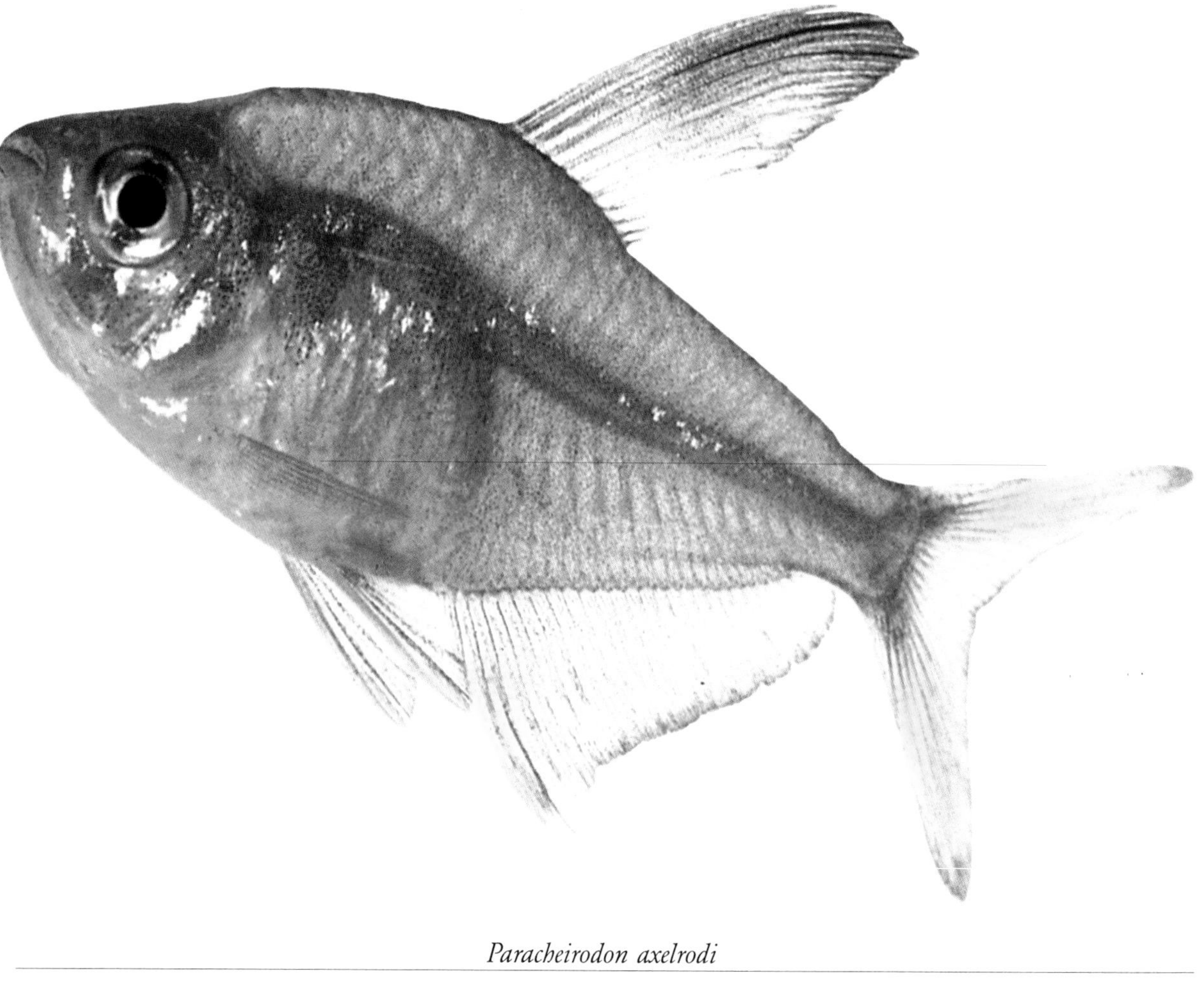

Paracheirodon axelrodi

Cardinal Tetra

➤ *Very extensively distributed in South America* ➤ *2 in (5 cm)* ➤ *73° to 81°F (23° to 27°C)*
Peaceful and gregarious

This is one of the most popular and widely sold fish in the world. Like its human counterpart, this cardinal wears purple and is blessed with a serene disposition. A significant stock of Cardinal Tetras still comes from the fishing grounds—that is, from the Rio Negro and from the Orinoco—but for several years another stock has been raised in Eastern Europe, where this tetra breeds very well. This gregarious fish dislikes harsh light and overly hard water. The Cardinal Tetra relishes Tubifex worms, black worms, or any other suitably sized live food.

Hyphessobrycon erythrostigma

Bleeding-heart Tetra

➤ *Colombia*
➤ *$2\frac{1}{3}$ to 3 in (6 to 8 cm)*
➤ *73° to 81°F (23° to 27°C)*
Peaceful

It is the striking red spot along its flank that has given rise to the name of this handsome fish. This robust, easygoing fish is originally from Colombia. Sexual dimorphism is obvious: The very long dorsal fin of the male ends with a plume. Comfortable in water that is 77°F (25°C), this tetra likes live food but will take flake food readily. This fish can be bred in a large aquarium.

Nematobrycon palmeri

Emperor Tetra

➤ *Colombia* ➤ *2 in (5 cm)* ➤ *73° to 79°F (23° to 26°C)*
Calm

Like its cousin the Black Phantom Tetra, the Emperor Tetra has a dorsal fin that is more developed in the male of the species. Since its original territory is the numerous rivers that flow into the Pacific Ocean, it is less demanding than other tetras about the acid content of its water. A neutral pH and water that is rather hard suit it well. In order to help it keep its characteristic spots, you should take care to reproduce its natural environment by planting the aquarium with thick vegetation, through which it can move freely, and by reducing the ambient light. The Emperor Tetra loves to eat worms and insects.

Megalamphodus megalopterus

Black Phantom Tetra

➤ *Brazil*
➤ *1 1/2 in (4 cm)*
➤ *73° to 79°F (23° to 26°C)*
Sociable

Very elegant and hardy, the Black Phantom Tetra enjoys being in a group, and its peaceful character makes it an ideal resident for a community aquarium. The black dorsal fin, more prominent on the male than on the female, rises prominently from the male's head. The Black Phantom Tetra likes the velvety environment created by floating plants and slightly acid freshwater, reminiscent of its Brazilian origins. Even under the best conditions, successful breeding is not guaranteed.

Hemigrammus pulcher

Garnet Tetra, Pretty Tetra

➤ *Amazon* ➤ *2 in (5 cm)*
➤ *73° to 82°F (23° to 28°C)*
Calm and gregarious

Small in size at 2 in (5 cm), the Garnet Tetra enjoys swimming about in rather dense vegetation, reminiscent of its origins in the Amazon. Unless you acquire at least five of these handsome, peaceful, and very gregarious fish, they will lose the advantage of their attractive coloration, because when they are few in number, they feel vulnerable and fail to develop. Although it is omnivorous, this fish has a weakness for small live prey.

Inset: The sail-finned form of the Black Phantom Tetra.

Hemigrammus caudovittatus

Buenos Aires Tetra

➤ *Río de la Plata basin*
➤ *3 to 4 in (8 to 10 cm)*
➤ *64° to 82°F (18° to 28°C)*
Peaceful and playful

For the beginning collector, the Buenos Aires Tetra is an excellent bridge between the goldfish and the tropical fish. This is because it is one of the hardiest fish. It does not require heated water, tolerating gradual temperature changes even as great as plus or minus 27°F (15°C), and can adapt to running water. A resident of the tank without any special dietary needs, this tetra has a nearly unlimited appetite. It eats nearly everything, even plants with tender shoots, which supplement its diet. It will not, however, eat the fins of its tankmates, even though its playful temperament will lead it to nibble at them on occasion. Although angelfish and others with long trailing fins risk seeing these appendages shortened when in the company of this tetra, it is not an aggressive fish. Indeed, it can even be put in with goldfish without any worries. This tet adapts well in aquariums. Both its life span and its breeding capacity are remarkable.

Hyphessobrycon pulchripinnis

Lemon Tetra

➤ *Amazon basin*
➤ *1½ to 2 in (4 to 5 cm)*
➤ *73° to 82°F (23° to 28°C)*
Peaceful

Boasting the same size as the Garnet Tetra, the Lemon Tetra can be distinguished by its anal fin, which is brightly colored brilliant yellow and black, especially in the case of the male. The dorsal fin, too, is more or less distinguished in the same way, depending on the individual fish. This attractive little freshwater fish enjoys swimming about in temperatures from 73° to 82°F (23° to 28°C).

Hyphessobrycon serpae

SERPAE

➤ *Paraguay, Mato Grosso* ➤ *$1\frac{1}{2}$ in (4 cm)* ➤ *72° to 82°F (22° to 28°C)*
Gregarious

Although the Serpae is a close relative of the Rosy Tetra, it is a beautiful shade of brilliant red that is better maintained. Its hardiness, relative immunity to diseases, and good appetite make it the ideal fish for beginning hobbyists. Nonetheless, although it is gregarious and peaceful, this tetra is unable to resist the temptation of nibbling at the fins of other fish, especially if they are smaller. Small neons are the ideal victims of the Serpae, and the Serpae profit considerably by changing territory. Breeding remains difficult in the aquarium.

Gymnocorymbus ternetzi

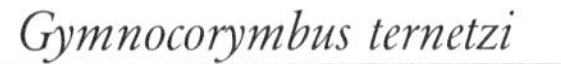

Black Tetra

➤ *Very widely distributed in South America* ➤ *$2\frac{1}{3}$ to 3 in (6 to 8 cm)*
➤ *72° to 79°F (22° to 26°C)*
Very peaceful

This attractive little fish has what looks like a mourning veil on its very long caudal fin, which is black during its youth and grows clearer with age. Along its sides, two large black streaks emphasize the somber appearance of this gentle fish. Despite its severe appearance, it is nonetheless extemely good-natured. It is also hardy–temperature is not critical, and it is not finicky about the water quality, or about the vegetation and food, except while breeding. Although nonaggressive, it defends itself against other aggressors. It is very prolific and long-lived.

Phenacogrammus interruptus

Congo Tetra

➤ *Congo basin* ➤ *Male: 3 in (8 cm); female: $2\frac{1}{3}$ in (6 cm)* ➤ *75° to 79°F (24° to 26°C)*
Peaceful

Sexual dimorphism is easily observed in the Congo Tetra: The male has a white dorsal fin that terminates in a point. This fish is generally peaceful, even timid. Small living prey are the favorite dish of this omnivore. Water at 79°F (26°C) that is soft and acid, makes this fish happy and ready for breeding. Oddly enough, this fish is not in great demand because its colors, like those of the rainbowfish, are rarely shown off to their advantage. In a community tank without the right lighting, it will appear sadly ordinary. But if properly lighted, its colors are spectacular.

Serrasalmidae

A close relative of the Characidae, this family of fish includes the piranha, a fish which embodies the terror of the collective unconscious. Tales of entire cows being devoured by fierce piranhas abound.

Colossoma bidens

RED-BELLIED PACU

➤ *Brazil, Bolivia* ➤ *15 $^2/_3$ to 17 $^1/_2$ in (40 to 45 cm)* ➤ *72° to 79°F (22° to 26°C)*
Mainly herbivorous

This fish is a close relative of the infamous piranha. It also has teeth, but its jaws are not as massive as those of the piranha. Unlike that of its cousin, however, the pacu's diet is made up mostly of vegetable matter. The fish eagerly eats ripened fruit that has fallen from trees whose branches overhang the rivers in which it lives. On their sides the young have black spots that fade as the fish matures. The red color under the jaw, gills, and belly remains throughout life. Purchased when young, this fish thrives in the aquarium. Pacus like to swim in schools, but even one fish kept singly requires a very large aquarium. Although the pacu is interesting and personable, significant thought should be given before acquiring this fish and the inevitable problem housing it will eventually cause.

Balitoridae

The fish of this family have a mouth that, over the course of time, has been transformed into a suction cup so powerful that it is difficult to remove it from off its anchorage. In the aquarium, they suck the algae that grow on the walls and the decorative fixtures.

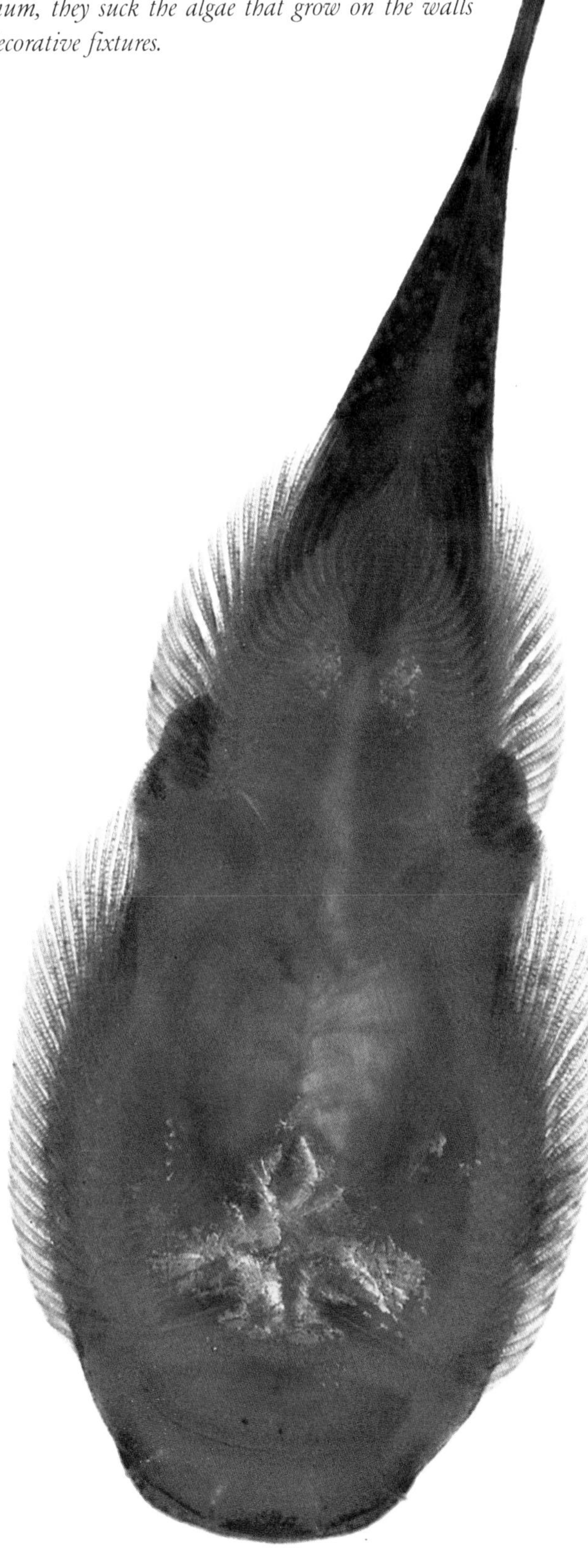

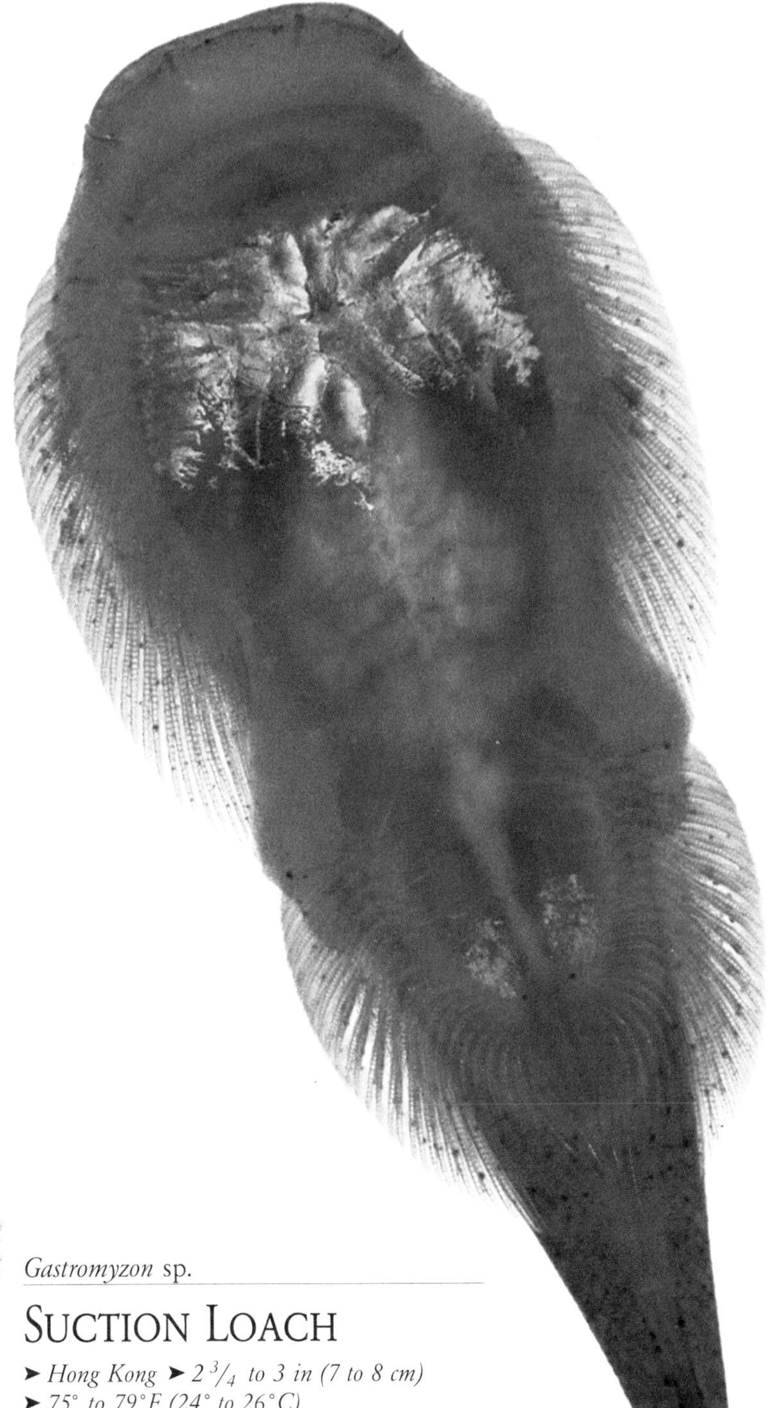

Gastromyzon sp.

Suction Loach

➤ *Hong Kong* ➤ *2 3/4 to 3 in (7 to 8 cm)*
➤ *75° to 79°F (24° to 26°C)*
Peaceful

This fish spends most of its time stuck to the glass walls of the tank, the rocks, and plant leaves. Always anchored to something, this little fish does not like moving very much. This is not to say that it remains inactive; indeed, far from it. It scrapes the decor and, by so doing, it feeds itself. This Asian species is particularly interesting to watch swimming about the aquarium. Always peaceful, the Suction Loach does not become aggressive as it ages. Like other catfish, it is difficult to net due to a series of small hooks on the side of its body. A white net with finer mesh prevents these hooks from catching on the material.

Callichthyidae

These freshwater tropical species, which are raised in aquariums worldwide, live exclusively on the bottom. There, these scaleless fish, armed with bony plates, spend the greater part of their time scouring the sandy floor. Very sociable and peaceful, they must occasionally rise to the surface of the water in order to snatch a mouthful of air.

Below: The Panda Corydoras, which has no sexual dimorphism.

Corydoras oiapoquensis

CORYDORAS CATFISH

➤ *Oyapock (French Guiana), Brazil* ➤ *2 1/3 in (6 cm)* ➤ *79°F (26°C)*
Very sociable and peaceful

This corydoras is a fish with many positive or pleasing characteristics. It is charming to look at in an aquarium, it has no problem living with other fish, and with its armored scales it is well protected against predators. This fish is also useful. Constantly rummaging about in the gravel, it prevents the substrate from packing down and thereby promotes the oxygenation of the bed of the tank. Unlike the hatchetfish, which eats food only from the surface, the *C. oiapoquensis* eats only from the bottom of the aquarium. It is particularly fond of living prey, especially *Tubifex* worms, and also eats granular and flake foods. Although this South American fish prefers slightly acid water, it is able to adapt itself to almost anything. The corydoras is also a fish that enjoys living in the company of others of its kind.

Corydoras axelrodi

Corydoras Catfish

- *Río Meta (Colombia)*
- *2 in (5 cm)*
- *75° to 79°F (24° to 26°C)*

Gregarious

This gregarious and peaceful corydoras also enjoys spending its time on the bottom of the aquarium, which it ceaselessly scours in search of food. In captivity, even if it is willing to eat dry food, it nonetheless longs for the *Tubifex* worms that it used to unearth when living in the wild. Sexual differentiation can be noted by the fact that the spines of the fins are longer on the male than on the female.

Corydoras paleatus

Peppered Corydoras

➤ *Northern South America* ➤ *2 3/4 in (7 cm)* ➤ *64° to 72°F (18° to 22°C)*
Peaceful

There are three related corydoras: the Peppered Corydoras (with very clear lateral streaks), the Three-striped Corydoras (*C. trilineatus*), and the Black-spotted Corydoras (*C. melanistius*), also called the Guiana Cat, which is sprinkled with very tiny black spots. All the corydoras have pectoral and dorsal fins, the first spine of which is in the shape of a thorn and is best not to seize bare-handed. Robust and hardy in most kinds of water, these fish enjoy small *Tubifex* worms more than anything else.

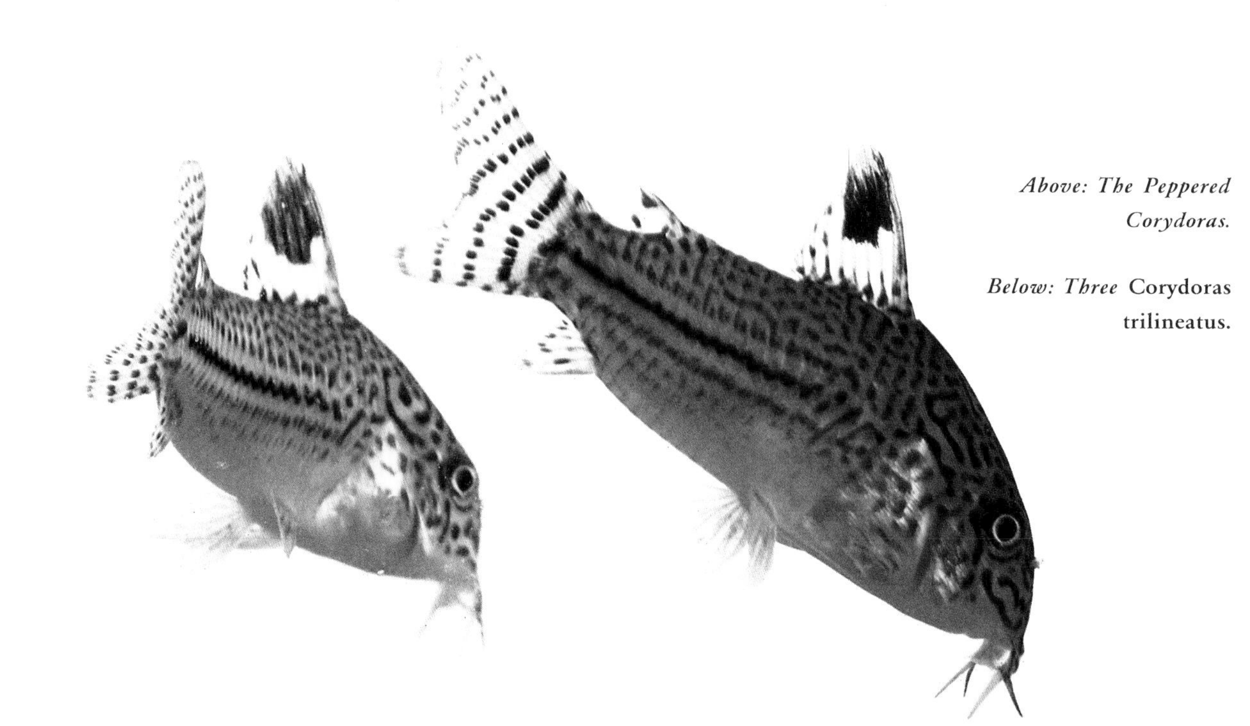

Above: The Peppered Corydoras.

Below: Three Corydoras trilineatus.

Above: Two albino corydoras with stocky bodies and an arched dorsal line.

Below: The Corydoras melanistius, *sprinkled with black spots.*

Loricariidae

These very popular fish have amassed a number of nicknames in recognition of their utility: algae eaters, sucker mouths, window washers. Commercially, the most common species of these scavengers is the "plecostomus" *(a name that has been erroneously used to designate a number of different species of* Hypostomus*). This fish ends up growing to an unwieldy size, making it poorly suited to the majority of aquariums. Moreover, its markings are somber and unglamorous. The example presented here, however, has a skin with varied tints, and its size remains entirely acceptable. Industrious and effective in their task of cleaning the glass sides of the aquarium, these fish have only one fault: their high price.*

Hypancistus zebra

ZEBRA PLECO

➤ *Amazon basin* ➤ *2 3/4 to 4 in (7 to 10 cm)* ➤ *79° to 82°F (26° to 28°C)*
Peaceful

Since its recent introduction to the fish hobbyist's market, it has been one of the most popular, thanks mostly to the beauty of its markings and its relatively modest size. Zebra Plecos should be fed zucchini strips along with romaine lettuce and other dark greens. *Tubifex* and black worms should also be offered. These fish are peaceful with other fish but aggressive to members of their own species. For this reason, it is best to keep only one in a tank. Despite its price, which is still rather high, this "new" fish should meet with the favor of collectors. Before receiving its classification in 1991, it was imported under the name "L.46."

Siluridae

Whereas the majority of the members of this family have a life that is strictly linked to the subsoil, the Glass Catfish and its close relatives live and swim about in the water.

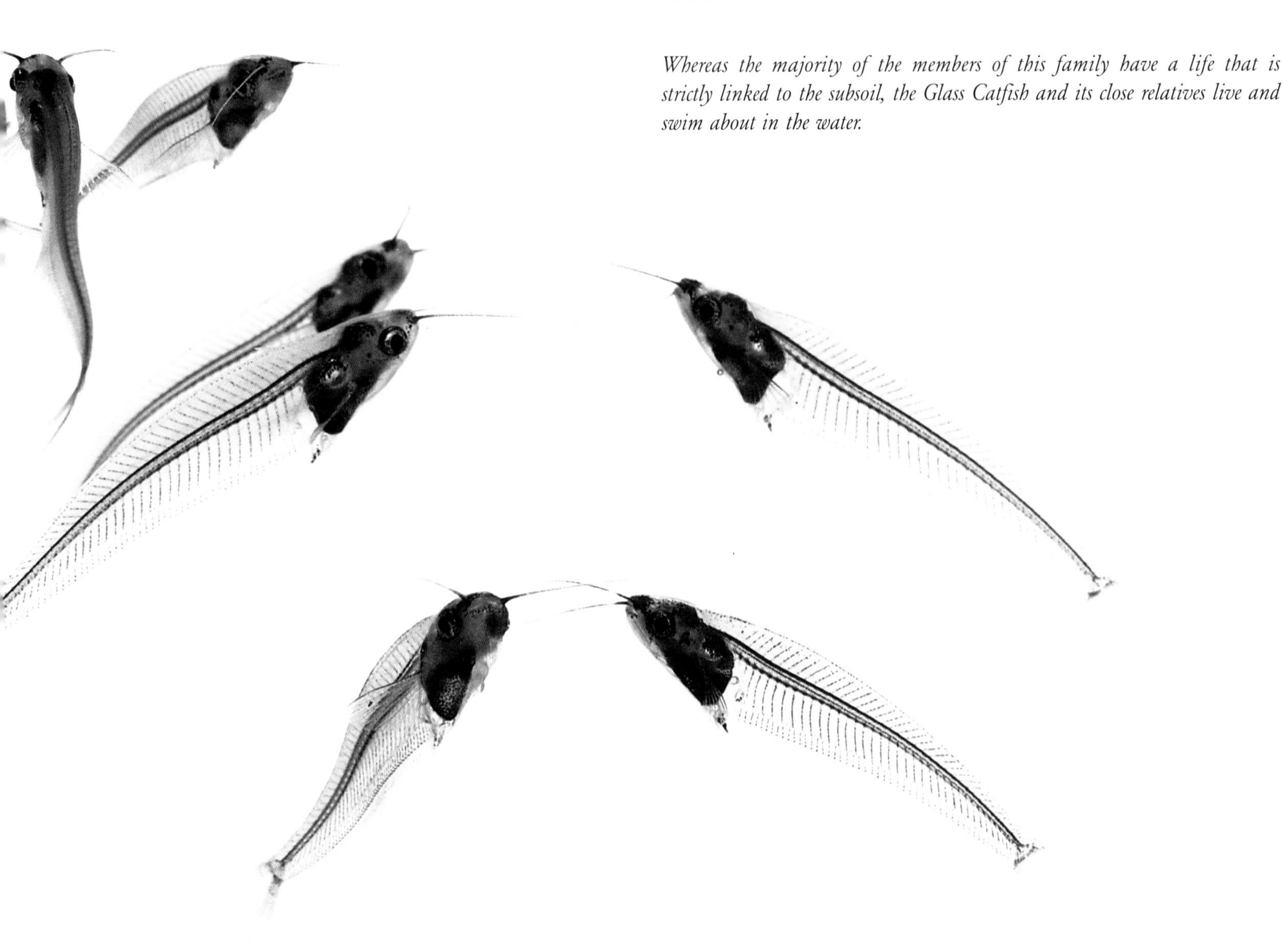

Kryptopterus bicirrhis

Glass Catfish

➤ *Southeast Asia* ➤ *4 in (10 cm)*
➤ *75° to 79°F (24° to 26°C)*
Very sociable

The skin of this fish is devoid of pigmentation and has the fragile transparency of crystal. One can even look through the body and distinguish its bones. Only the head and the stomach cavity are gray. In order for it to display subtle reflections that range from green to pink, it is necessary for you to create a region of half shadow in the aquarium. Adding several plants on the surface will help the Glass Catfish feel at home, especially during the delicate period of its adaptation to the tank. If you wish to indulge in an amusing experiment, all you need to do is give the fish some live food, such as mosquito larvae, and before your very eyes the uninterrupted digestive process can be seen, without disturbing the fish in the least.

Pangasiidae

During their youth, the large-sized swimmers that constitute this family enjoy nothing so much as schooling and living in a group. If isolated, they tend to waste away. On the other hand, once fully grown, they are rather solitary.

Pangasius sutchi

IRIDESCENT SHARK

➤ *Thailand* ➤ *6 to 18 in (15 to 46 cm), depending on the size of aquarium*
➤ *72° to 77°F (22° to 25°C)*
Gregarious

Tapered like a shark, this large fish requires a very long aquarium of large volume. During its youth, it swims all the time in a school yet remains solitary when it reaches adulthood. It is an active fish, always in motion. This fish prefers to hunt when young, then, progressively losing its teeth, it passes the remainder of its days as a herbivore.

Cyprinodontidae

Found on every continent except Australia, these attractive toothed fish live in nearly any kind of water (with a few rare exceptions), whether it is still or running. The development of their eggs can either be continuous (as with other fish) or discontinuous; that is, after spawning they are buried in the soil, which periodically dries out. These eggs must then wait several months before the rains arrive to make them hatch. Though some species are extremely beautiful aquarium fish, many are aggressive and should not be kept in a community tank situation.

Nothobranchius guentheri

GÜNTHER'S NOTHOBRANCH, GÜNTHER'S FIRE KILLIFISH

➤ *Eastern Africa*
➤ *1 1/2 to 2 3/4 in (4 to 7 cm)*
➤ *68° to 75°F (20° to 24°C)*
Aggressive

Luckily, this small African fish has the advantage of being very attractive. On the downside, it is small in size (its body is longer than wide) and has an aggressive temperament. As a result, life in a community tank is difficult, all the more so because it needs water of a very specific character: lightly acid with low mineral content. In defense of this fish, though, we must add that it knows how to live contentedly in a small aquarium, indeed even in a simple tank with a bit of sand on the bottom and a pretty plant–all without a heating unit. However, avoid overly powerful filtration. Sexual dimorphism is very obvious. The male has beautiful colors that vary between bright red and blue, passing through green and the whole spectrum of the rainbow. Distinctly more drab, the female makes do with a color that is dull brown.

Aphyosemion australe

LYRETAIL

➤ *Gabon* ➤ *2 in (5 cm)* ➤ *68° to 73°F (20° to 23°C)*
Peaceful

The male, depending on the variety, enjoys displaying his handsome brilliant markings with blue-green reflections spattered with red spots; the female has a duller complexion, a dull beige that is nonetheless enlivened with a few red spots. This calm and peaceful fish can make do with a small, shallow aquarium under one condition: The tank must be covered with a lid, as the fish is an excellent jumper. Despite its equatorial origins, it does better in cooler water.

Poeciliidae

Along with the family Characidae, the Poeciliidae constitute the largest source for stocking aquariums. Mostly of Central American origin, but also from the islands surrounding South America, these fish are ovoviviparous; that is, the eggs, which are fertilized in the female by the introduction of the male gonopodium, hatch shortly before birth, or actually while being expelled. For those seeking easy breeding possibilities, this presents a certain interest. For the most part, these fish now come from Asian hatcheries, which explains their recent adaptation to freshwater with a slightly acid pH. Nonetheless, a supplement of salt for specimens coming from brackish water or estuaries is useful, especially for breeding. Fish enthusiasts derive the greatest pleasure from the infinite variety of this species' forms and colors.

Poecilia latipinna

Lyretail Black Molly

➤ *Central America*
➤ *$2\frac{3}{4}$ to $3\frac{1}{2}$ in (7 to 9 cm)*
➤ *77° to 82°F (25° to 28°C)*
Active

Whether the variant is marbled, yellow-marbled, or all black as shown here, the Lyretail Black Molly is a hardy creature that lives in hard water–it is an active fish and demonstrates this in the aquarium, which should be spacious. As for its water (alkaline), a pinch of salt would not be unwelcome. The amorous exchanges of this ovoviviparous fish resemble the sparring of boxers, and the offspring of these exchanges, although numerous, will not all survive to see the light of day. Remove the fry from the greedy reach of their parents as soon as they are born. They accept flake food from a very early age and, as they begin to grow older, they will eat live food.

Poecilia latipinna

Black Molly variations

➤ *Central America* ➤ *2 3/4 to 3 1/2 in (7 to 9 cm)* ➤ *77° to 82°F (25° to 28°C)*
Active and tolerant

Some of the numerous varieties of the Black Molly, these are very active fish, which should only be kept in an aquarium inhabited by other species that are just as active and that tolerate very hard, warm, and slightly salty water.

Successive hybridization has enabled breeders to obtain a great many variants of color and shape, including the Poecilia latipinna *(left) or the* P. velifera *(opposite page).*

Poecilia velifera

SAILFIN MOLLY

- ➤ *Mexico*
- ➤ *4 ²/₃ in (12 cm) in the aquarium*
- ➤ *73° to 79°F (23° to 26°C)*

Peaceful with fish its own size

Individuals of both sexes have a dorsal fin that seems joined to the caudal fin, and so they are rigged like a sailboat. They are brackish-water fish and are sometimes even spotted by swimmers diving in coral reefs, where they may display two kinds of behavior. Either they are busy searching endlessly for some food at the bottom of the sea, coming and going, digging about in the sand, or else they are swimming about peacefully among the rocks and the other fish, meandering at a thoroughly nonchalant pace, gracefully extending their large fins like ballet dancers. Everything about their languorous pace makes the viewer think of a dance.

Xiphophorus variatus

VARIEGATED PLATY

➤ *Mexico* ➤ *1 1/2 to 2 3/4 in (4 to 7 cm), depending on the variety; the female is larger than the male* ➤ *73°F (23°C)*
Very peaceful

Here is one of the numerous mutations of *Xiphophorus* produced through selective breeding. Its colored flanks range from yellow to green and are sometimes spangled with dark spots. It can also possess ornamental sail-like dorsal fins. The aquarium should contain plenty of plants, and the pH of the water should be slightly alkaline. The temperature can vary between 68° and 75°F (20° and 24°C). The fish is also a prolific breeder.

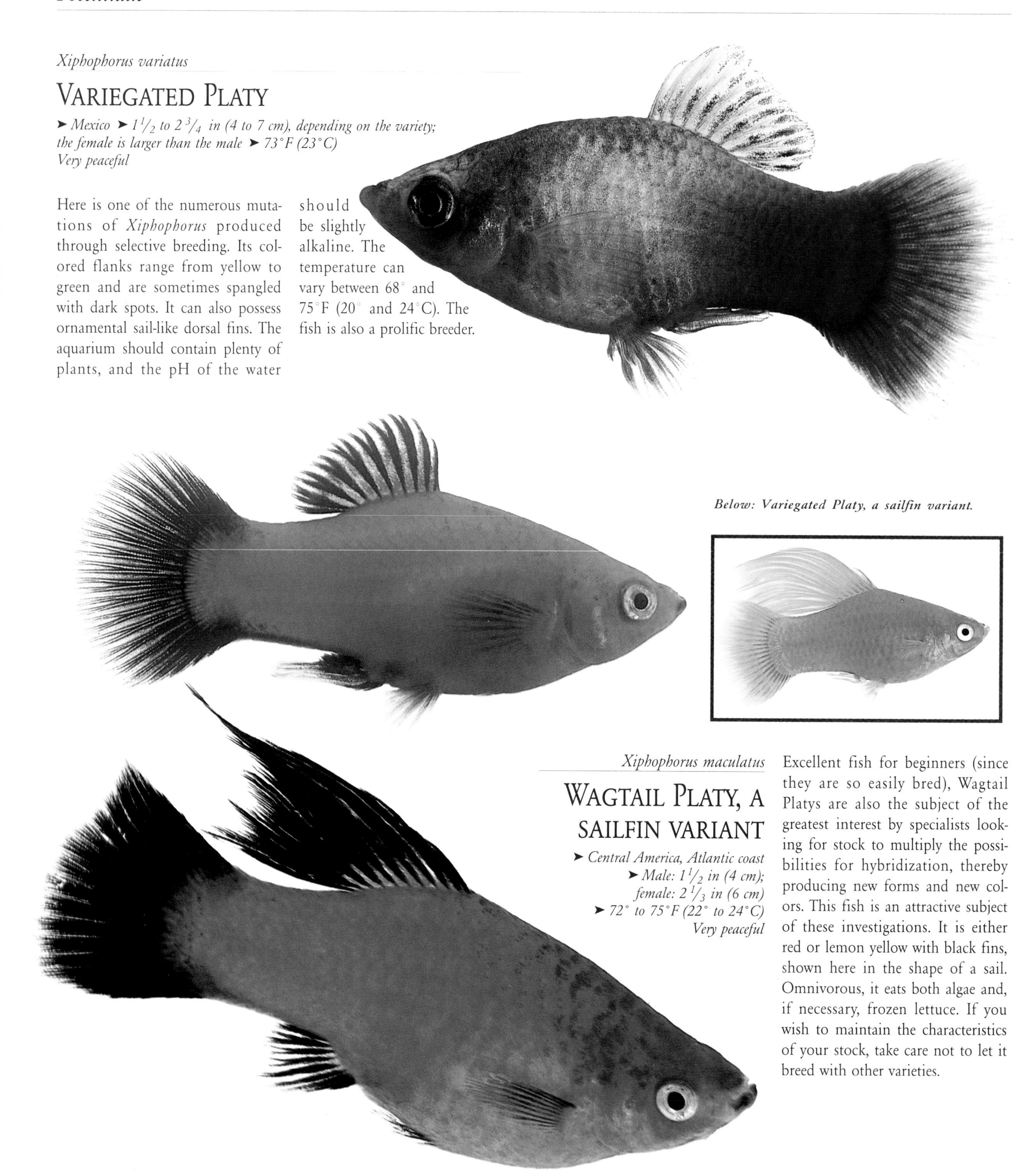

Below: Variegated Platy, a sailfin variant.

Xiphophorus maculatus

WAGTAIL PLATY, A SAILFIN VARIANT

➤ *Central America, Atlantic coast*
➤ *Male: 1 1/2 in (4 cm); female: 2 1/3 in (6 cm)*
➤ *72° to 75°F (22° to 24°C)*
Very peaceful

Excellent fish for beginners (since they are so easily bred), Wagtail Platys are also the subject of the greatest interest by specialists looking for stock to multiply the possibilities for hybridization, thereby producing new forms and new colors. This fish is an attractive subject of these investigations. It is either red or lemon yellow with black fins, shown here in the shape of a sail. Omnivorous, it eats both algae and, if necessary, frozen lettuce. If you wish to maintain the characteristics of your stock, take care not to let it breed with other varieties.

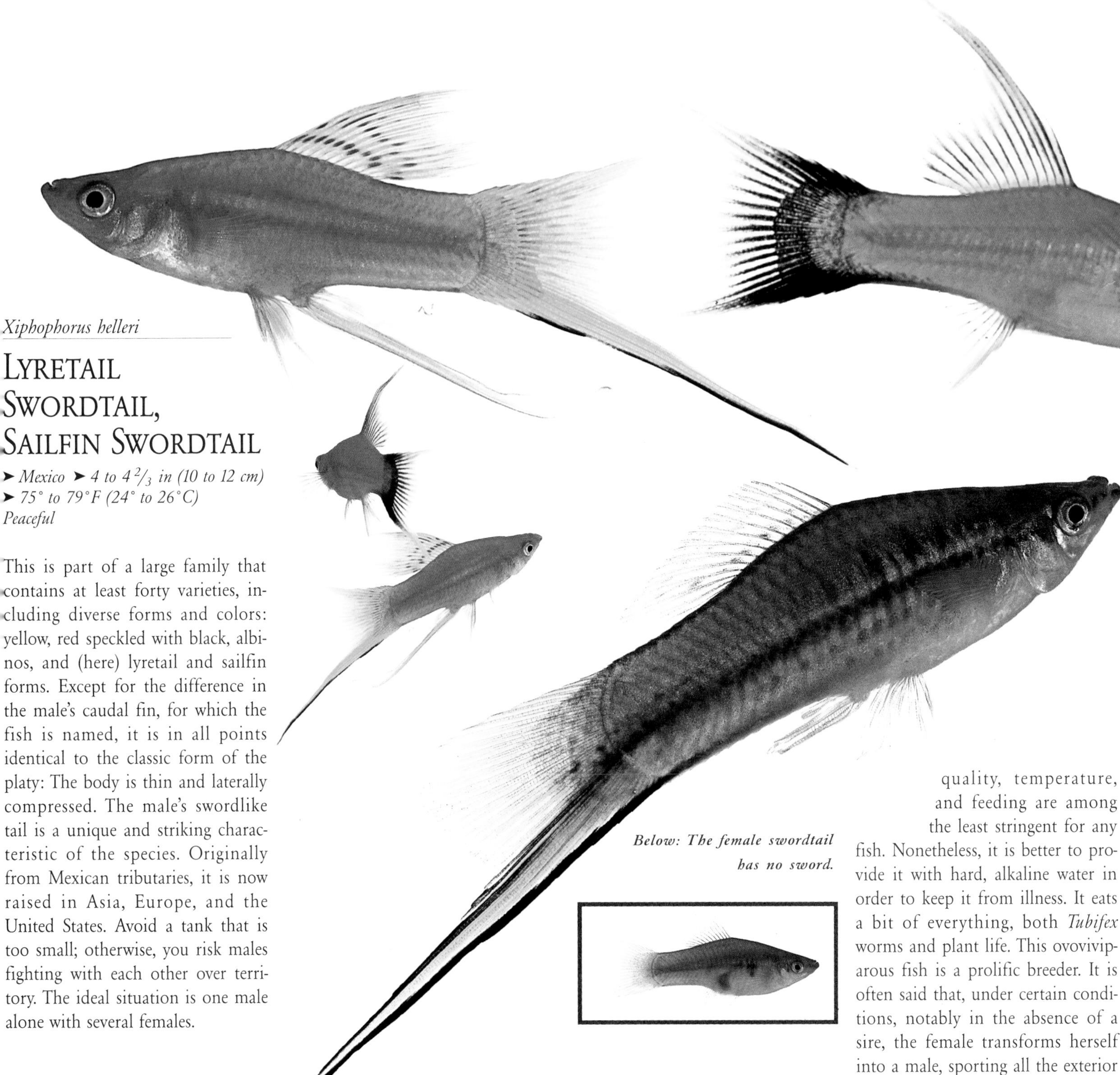

Xiphophorus helleri

Lyretail Swordtail, Sailfin Swordtail

➤ *Mexico* ➤ *4 to 4 2/3 in (10 to 12 cm)*
➤ *75° to 79°F (24° to 26°C)*
Peaceful

This is part of a large family that contains at least forty varieties, including diverse forms and colors: yellow, red speckled with black, albinos, and (here) lyretail and sailfin forms. Except for the difference in the male's caudal fin, for which the fish is named, it is in all points identical to the classic form of the platy: The body is thin and laterally compressed. The male's swordlike tail is a unique and striking characteristic of the species. Originally from Mexican tributaries, it is now raised in Asia, Europe, and the United States. Avoid a tank that is too small; otherwise, you risk males fighting with each other over territory. The ideal situation is one male alone with several females.

Below: The female swordtail has no sword.

Xiphophorus helleri

Swordtail

➤ *Mexico* ➤ *4 to 4 2/3 in (10 to 12 cm)*
➤ *75° to 79°F (24° to 26°C)*
Peaceful

Only the male swordtail bears the rapier, which enables it to overtake the female length by several millimeters. Originally this fish had green markings, then, as a result of selective breeding varieties arose that were red, orange, sometimes even black. At the same time, in some cases, the caudal fin assumed the shape of a lyre, or the dorsal fin took on the shape of a sail. The swordtail is a good fish for beginners since the constraints of water quality, temperature, and feeding are among the least stringent for any fish. Nonetheless, it is better to provide it with hard, alkaline water in order to keep it from illness. It eats a bit of everything, both *Tubifex* worms and plant life. This ovoviviparous fish is a prolific breeder. It is often said that, under certain conditions, notably in the absence of a sire, the female transforms herself into a male, sporting all the exterior signs of her newfound fortune: gonopodium and sword, instead of a fan-shaped tail, and most important, fertility. Such a metamorphosis, though, has not yet been verified. It seems instead that certain fish are late-blooming males, who exhibit the characteristics of the female for a protracted period before arriving at sexual maturity.

Poecilia reticulata

GUPPY

➤ *Northern South America* ➤ *Male: 1 in (3 cm); female: 2 in (5 cm)* ➤ *68° to 77°F (20° to 25°C)*
Peaceful

This is the most popular species of this family of fish and one of the most popular aquarium fish. Its size, which enables it to live in small aquariums, as well as its infinite variety of shapes and colors all help it entice both beginning fish enthusiasts and seasoned aquarists. In addition, it is easy to breed. The species was described in 1859 by a German scientist named Wilhelm Peters. It was imported into Europe at the end of the nineteenth century by Dr. Robert Guppy, an English botanist who brought preserved specimens to England. An ichthyologist at the British Museum thought it was a new species and named it after Guppy. In nature, it does not exhibit the same characteristics as those that can be admired today in community tanks. In the wild, the fish are less strikingly colored and exhibit more modest fins. In captivity, they have, with the assistance of selective breeding, developed other finery; colors and size have been enhanced. The male, half the size of his companion, nonetheless has a very clear advantage: His markings are richer and his caudal fin is much more developed. Both male and female, though, share the same sociable temperament. Wild guppies are hardy fish adapted to living in all kinds of environments, from freshwater to brackish water. They are happy anywhere, even when temperature differences vary by as much as 18°F (10°C). Be careful, though, with tank-raised strains, which are a great deal more fragile. These omnivorous fish accept all kinds of food.

This polymorphous species displays considerable variations in both markings and shape.

Poecilia reticulata

Metallic Blue Guppy

➤ *Breeder-raised guppy* ➤ *Male: 1 in (3 cm); female: 2 1/3 in (6 cm)*
➤ *68° to 77°F (20° to 25°C)*
Peaceful

Guppies are easy to breed. A single fertilization by the male is enough to produce two or three litters. Four to six weeks after mating, depending on the temperature, the first fry appear. If you wish to save them, two techniques are possible. The first, a natural method, consists of furnishing the aquarium with a number of plants, which protect the young from the voracious appetites of their parents. The other consists of placing the pregnant female in a small aquarium so as to isolate the fry from the predatory temptations of their parents. Do not place the mother in a birthing tank; she will be too stressed. One thing that is astonishing is the ability of the female, when placed in a hostile environment, to delay or slow down her spawning if the survival of her young is threatened.

Belontiidae

The fish in this family belong to the suborder Anabantoidei and can be referred to as anabantids. The Belontiidae as well as the other fish included in this suborder live in the freshwaters of Asia and Africa and possess an unusual anatomical feature: a labyrinth, the supplementary respiratory organ located behind the eyes, which enables them to breathe at the water's surface. Most anabantids use their gills less often than other fish. This fact allows them to thrive in stagnant, polluted waters where other fish would perish.

Trichogaster leeri

Pearl Gourami

➤ *Borneo, Sumatra, Malaysia* ➤ *4 in (10 cm)* ➤ *75° to 79°F (24° to 26°C)*
The calmest of the Belontiidae

The male has a very colorful throat and stomach, and his dorsal and anal fins are more streamlined than those of the female. Both sexes, though, have a magnificent pearly skin spangled with a multitude of brilliant spots. Their quiet temperament makes them a good companion for whatever fish they swim among. The Pearl Gourami is omnivorous. Although the fish is in no way finicky, it is not a bad idea to pamper it with small live prey. If well nourished and well cared for, it can live for more than eight years.

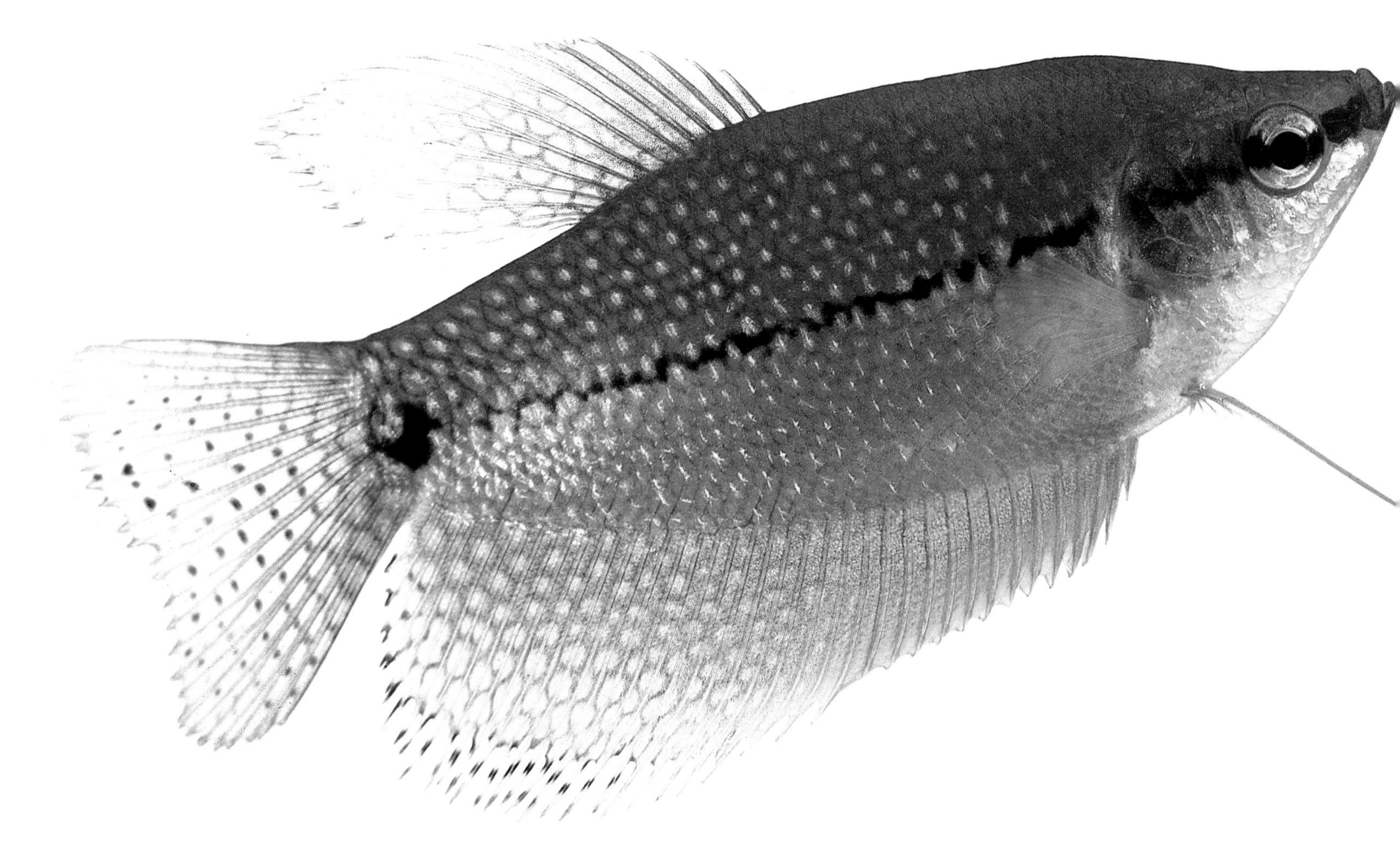

Colisa lalia

DWARF GOURAMI

➤ *India, Borneo* ➤ *2 in (5 cm)* ➤ *75° to 79°F (24° to 26°C)*
Peaceful

The Dwarf Gourami is one-third the size of the Gold Gourami. A magnificent though timid fish, it has the advantage of being very easily bred in the aquarium. Originally from the rice fields of India, this fish reproduces well in environments that promote evaporation and condensation. One can increase simple and rapid breeding by re-creating similar conditions: an aquarium with very little water (2 in, 5 cm), a piece of glass across the top of the tank to allow condensation to flow back into the aquarium, some floating plants, and a water temperature of 82°F (28°C). Once these conditions have been created, the urge to breed should soon follow. The male is colorful; the female, silvery. These omnivorous fish readily take small live prey as well as flake food.

Trichogaster trichopterus

BLUE GOURAMI

➤ *Southeast Asia*
➤ *3 to 4 in (8 to 10 cm) in the aquarium, 6 in (15 cm) in the wild*
➤ *79°F (26°C)*
Calm

Although the Blue Gourami is much more peaceful than the Gold Gourami, it is still necessary to avoid placing it with smaller fish. It has no difficulty reaching an understanding with other fish its own size in the aquarium. The wild specimens as well as certain domestic varieties are called Three-spotted Gouramis because of the dark spots that mark their sides and the caudal peduncle. To this description we may add mention of the black velvet of their irises, set against a bluish, delicately silvered ground. It is possible that this fish is such a success because of its beautiful coloration as well as its hardiness and easy and prolific breeding, which guarantees an ever-growing population.

Trichogaster trichopterus

Gold Gourami

➤ *Southeast Asia*
➤ *3 to 4 in (8 to 10 cm)*
➤ *79°F (26°C)*
Rather bellicose

The Gold Gourami is a variation of the Blue Gourami. It is a pseudo-albino morph of the original wild type that has gained great popularity. The male has a black dorsal fin terminating in a point, whereas the fin of the female is clearly rounded off in a fan shape. We should point out that the Gold Gourami is rather pugnacious in a community tank. Otherwise, it is as hardy as the blue form.

Betta splendens

BETTA, SIAMESE FIGHTING FISH

➤ *Thailand, Cambodia* ➤ *2 to 2 3/4 in (5 to 7 cm)* ➤ *75° to 86°F (24° to 30°C)*
Males among themselves: combative; females: more sociable

This solitary creature gets its name because it does not tolerate the presence of even a single member of its own species. It often reacts badly to other smaller, colorful species, especially those with long, flowing fins, because it mistakes them for other male bettas. Easy to keep with calm fish and with invertebrates, it enjoys living hidden in the nooks and crannies of the decor. Sexual dimorphism is obvious: On the male, the fins are very elongated; the female must content herself with more modest fins. Mating is a ritual that follows definite steps. First, the male builds a nest consisting of bubbles coated with saliva. Then, with all his fins extended, he approaches his chosen mate to court her. If she is receptive, she moves under the nest. Fertilized in the open water, the eggs are immediately gathered by the male in his mouth and deposited in the nest, which he will protect during the incubation period. However, after the birth is over, the natural combativeness of the fighter will rapidly resurface, and it is necessary to remove the parents in order to prevent the fry from having their lives dramatically shortened. The Siamese Fighting Fish accepts frozen animal food, and to help it feel at home in the tank, you should treat it to some small live prey.

The yellow Siamese Fighting Fish, above, has just succeeded in his attack. He has a piece of the blue Siamese Fighting Fish in his mouth. This is a good demonstration of what happens when the males are not kept apart.

Atherinidae

The Atherinidae have marine origins, which is why the majority of them—even those that now live in fresh or brackish water—will be more comfortable with a light supplement of sea salt, depending on their geographic origins. A closely related family, the Melanotaeniidae, were formerly grouped with the Atherinidae and also benefit from a sea salt supplement.

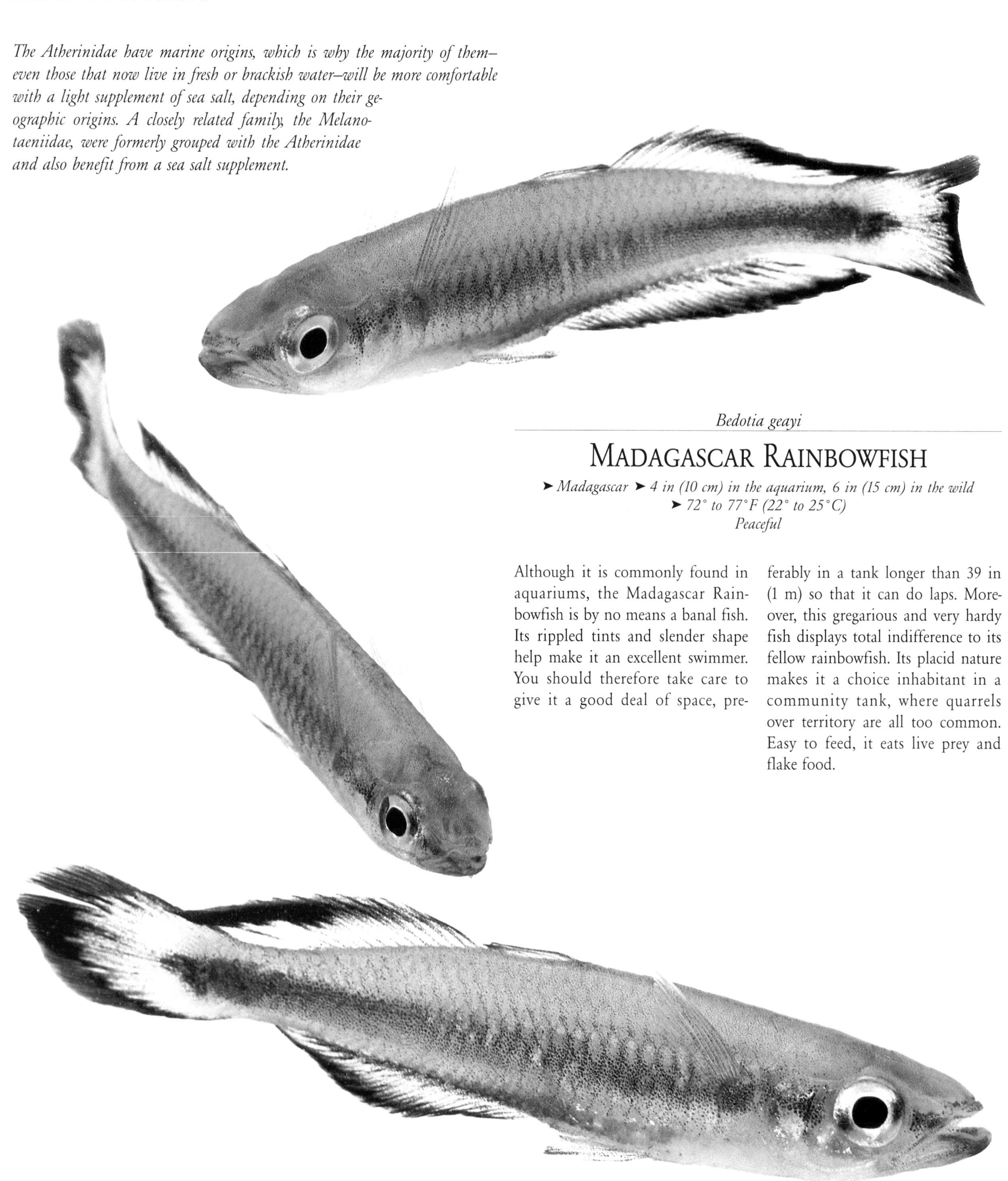

Bedotia geayi

Madagascar Rainbowfish

➤ *Madagascar* ➤ *4 in (10 cm) in the aquarium, 6 in (15 cm) in the wild*
➤ *72° to 77°F (22° to 25°C)*
Peaceful

Although it is commonly found in aquariums, the Madagascar Rainbowfish is by no means a banal fish. Its rippled tints and slender shape help make it an excellent swimmer. You should therefore take care to give it a good deal of space, preferably in a tank longer than 39 in (1 m) so that it can do laps. Moreover, this gregarious and very hardy fish displays total indifference to its fellow rainbowfish. Its placid nature makes it a choice inhabitant in a community tank, where quarrels over territory are all too common. Easy to feed, it eats live prey and flake food.

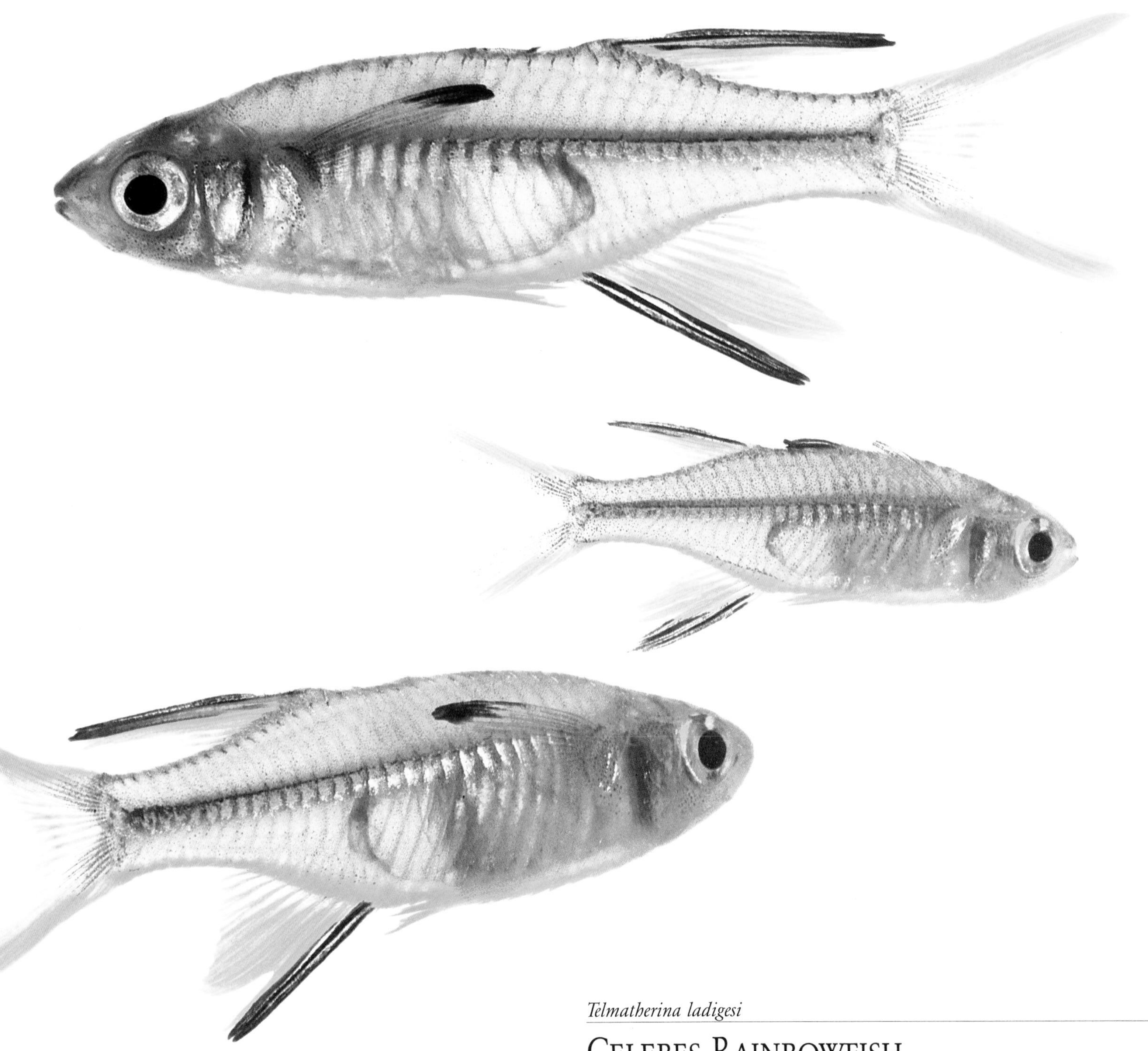

Telmatherina ladigesi

Celebes Rainbowfish

➤ *Celebes (Indonesia)* ➤ *$2\,^1/_3$ to $2\,^3/_4$ in (6 to 7 cm)* ➤ *77°F (25°C)*
Lively but peaceful

With its tapered body, its yellow coloration with an iridescent blue-green line, and its fins with disproportionately large rays, the male Celebes Rainbowfish are very beautiful to look at. The female is just a bit less graceful. They prefer to live in a group. The Celebes Rainbowfish requires hard water with a light supplement of sea salt. If possible, place the tank where the fishes' scales may catch the morning sun.

Melanotaeniidae

Sexual dimorphism is generally obvious in these fish, which originate mostly from Australia and New Guinea. The males are clearly larger and more deeply colored. As for breeding, they are very prolific.

Melanotaenia lacustris

Lake Kutubu Rainbowfish

➤ *Southern New Guinea*
➤ *3 to 4 ⅔ in (8 to 12 cm)*
➤ *77° to 81°F (25° to 27°C)*
Lively without aggressiveness

A close relative of the *M. maccullochi,* this rainbowfish matches it point for point in behavior, description, and care requirements. Only the coloration of the skin distinguishes them: The background color of the Lake Kutubu Rainbowfish is solid blue and more intense. However, if stressed or simply displaced from its natural habitat, the fish will indicate its dispiritedness by assuming a gray pallor. It is active and requires a large, open swimming place.

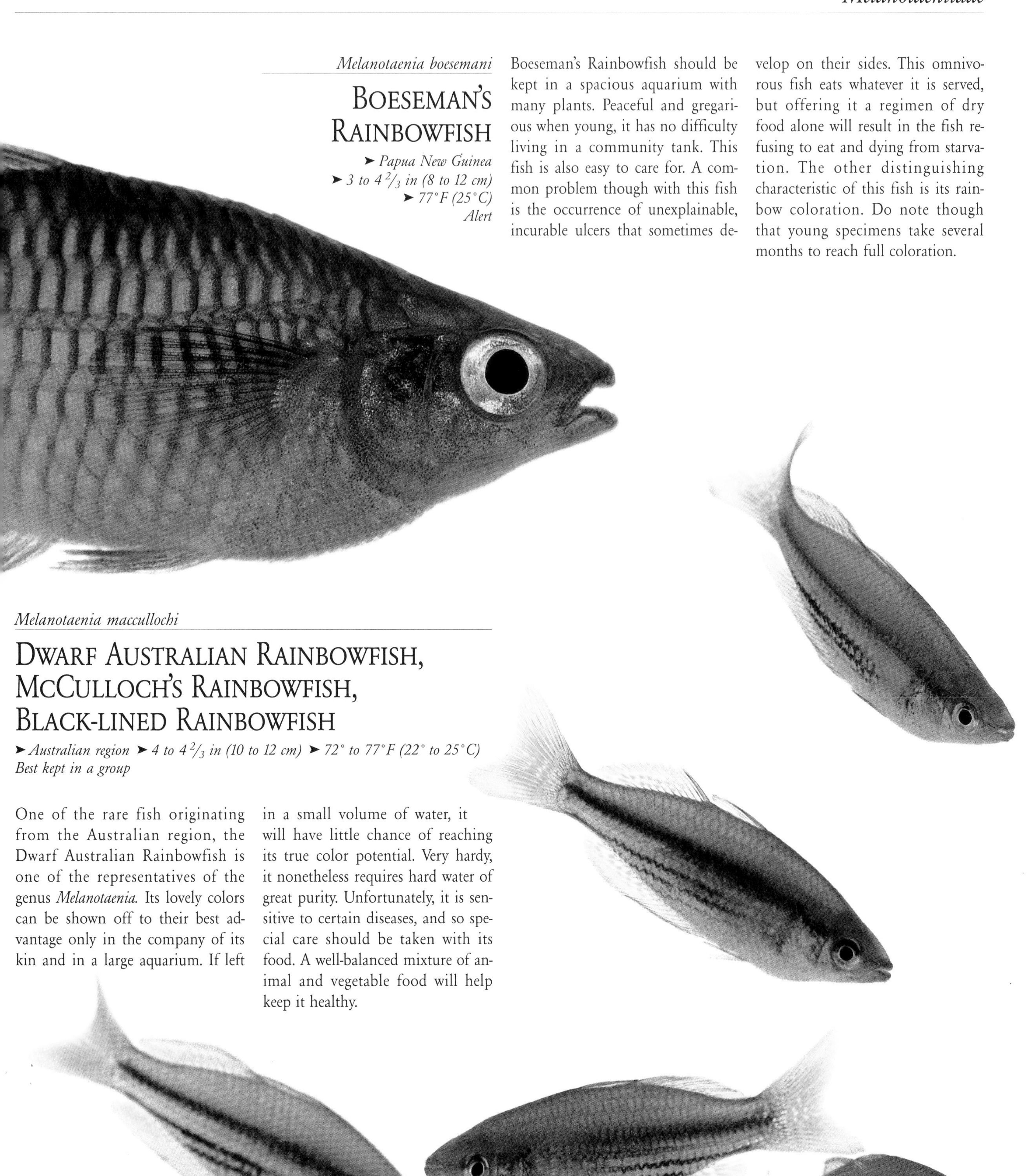

Melanotaenia boesemani

Boeseman's Rainbowfish

➤ *Papua New Guinea*
➤ *3 to 4 2/3 in (8 to 12 cm)*
➤ *77°F (25°C)*
Alert

Boeseman's Rainbowfish should be kept in a spacious aquarium with many plants. Peaceful and gregarious when young, it has no difficulty living in a community tank. This fish is also easy to care for. A common problem though with this fish is the occurrence of unexplainable, incurable ulcers that sometimes develop on their sides. This omnivorous fish eats whatever it is served, but offering it a regimen of dry food alone will result in the fish refusing to eat and dying from starvation. The other distinguishing characteristic of this fish is its rainbow coloration. Do note though that young specimens take several months to reach full coloration.

Melanotaenia maccullochi

Dwarf Australian Rainbowfish, McCulloch's Rainbowfish, Black-lined Rainbowfish

➤ *Australian region* ➤ *4 to 4 2/3 in (10 to 12 cm)* ➤ *72° to 77°F (22° to 25°C)*
Best kept in a group

One of the rare fish originating from the Australian region, the Dwarf Australian Rainbowfish is one of the representatives of the genus *Melanotaenia.* Its lovely colors can be shown off to their best advantage only in the company of its kin and in a large aquarium. If left in a small volume of water, it will have little chance of reaching its true color potential. Very hardy, it nonetheless requires hard water of great purity. Unfortunately, it is sensitive to certain diseases, and so special care should be taken with its food. A well-balanced mixture of animal and vegetable food will help keep it healthy.

Cichlidae

Native to the American and African continents and sometimes to Southeast Asia, cichlids generally display beautiful colors and unusual shapes. Their dorsal fins are frequently armed with hard spiny rays in the anterior portion. Usually peaceful among themselves, if their requirements are respected they have the additional advantage of being very prolific breeders and of taking the greatest care of their offspring. An aquarium housing only cichlids is recommended for the largest species, whereas the small Apistogramma *or* Aequidens *are suitable for a community tank.*

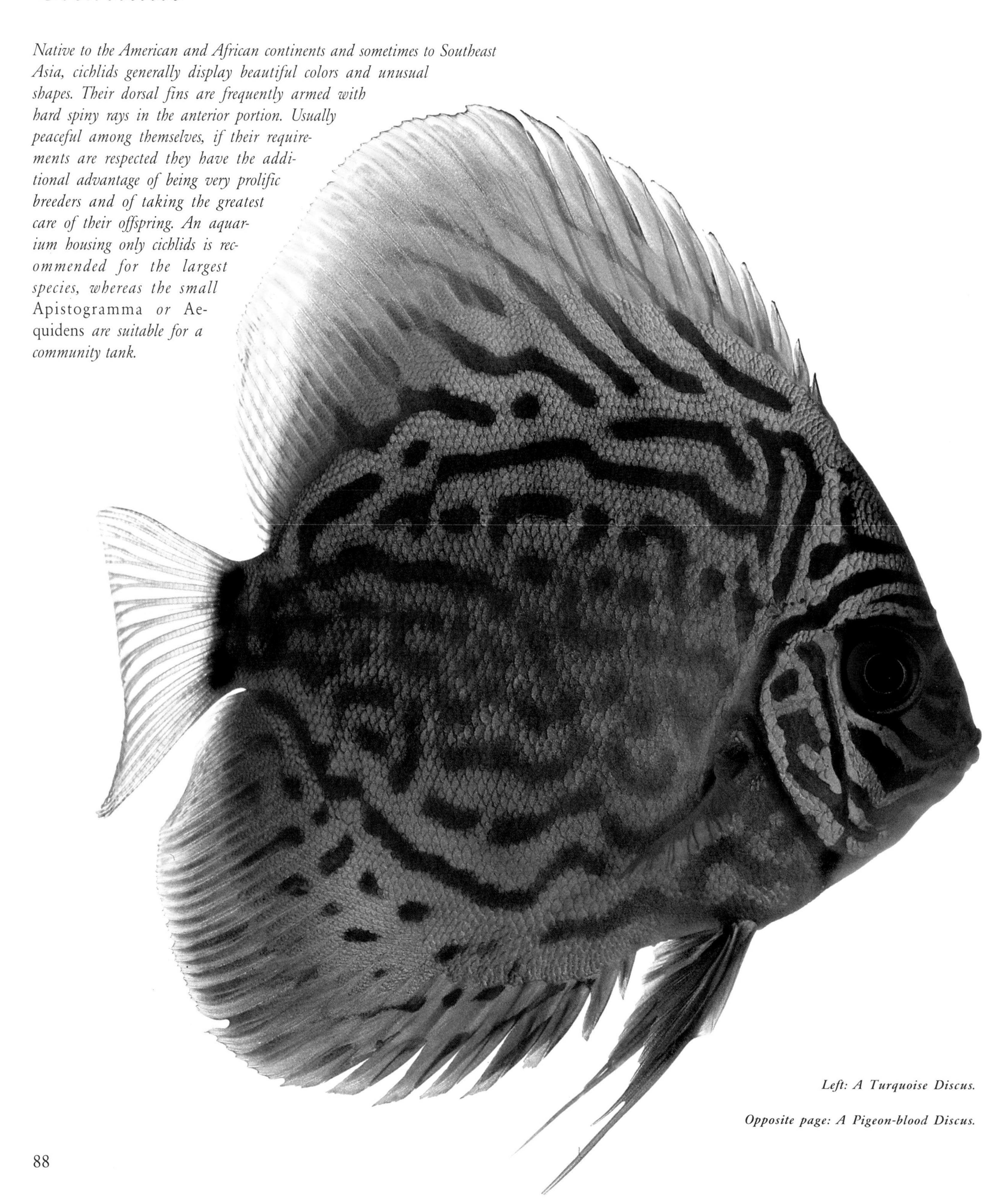

Left: A Turquoise Discus.

Opposite page: A Pigeon-blood Discus.

Symphysodon aequifasciata

Common Discus, Brown Discus

➤ *Amazon* ➤ *6 to 7 3/4 in (15 to 20 cm)* ➤ *79° to 86°F (26° to 30°C)*
Peaceful

This fish originally was found only in South America. It has since spread to all the Asian, European, and U.S. breeding farms, where selective breeding has given it its rich palette of colors (turquoise in the example shown, and sometimes cobalt). For several years, the capture of wild specimens has been intensified in order to satisfy the needs both of enthusiasts for pure stock and of professionals in search of new genetic stock for breeding yet more new varieties. This large fish (6 to 8 in, 15 to 20 cm) should be kept in water that is at least 82°F (28°C), with a low pH and density. Like the sloth, the discus does not tolerate a feverishly paced environment. Therefore, avoid placing it with rapid and fidgety fish, such as barbs; instead, the company of corydoras or cardinal tetras would be preferable. If the discus should become stressed, expect the fish to stop eating, get sick, and probably die. However, there are warning signals that indicate when the discus is feeling ill or adapting poorly—it turns dark. Two solutions are possible: Either change its aquarium, or boost the temperature of the water so that it reaches 90°F (32°C) and allow the fish to remain there for forty-eight hours.

Astronotus ocellatus

OSCAR

➤ *Amazon* ➤ *8 to 16 in (20 to 40 cm), depending on the size of the aquarium* ➤ *72° to 77°F (22° to 25°C)*
Predatory when young, hostile as an adult

Tiger Oscar.

The coloration of these large fish varies according to their evolutionary niche. The Tiger Oscar pictured here is entirely the product of selective breeding. Contrary to the nature of its original stock, where the attractive markings of the young disappear with the years as the fish assumes a predominately greenish shade, the Tiger Oscar attains an even more attractive coloration as an adult. Its large size requires a large tank indeed, all the more so since this fish is subject to abrupt mood swings for no apparent reason. With an appetite commensurate with its large body, it eats anything that can be swallowed.

Apistogramma cacatuoides

COCKATOO DWARF CICHLID, CRESTED DWARF CICHLID

➤ *South America* ➤ *Male: 2 1/3 in (6 cm); female: 1 to 2 in (3 to 5 cm)* ➤ *75° to 79°F (24° to 26°C)*
Territorial

This small and very colorful fish is aggressive and does not cease from quarreling with other members of its group. Since the male is polygamous, you can avoid difficulties by placing only one male per tank and providing him with at least three females. The male reigns over a hierarchically structured group, taking his meals before the females. This species is one of the rare *Apistogramma* able to live in hard water with a neutral pH. You will have no problems here with acidity or with stabilizing the water quality.

Haplochromis burtoni

Burton's Mouthbreeder

➤ *Lake Tanganyika, Lake Kivu, and their estuaries* ➤ *Male: 4 to 4 2/3 in (10 to 12 cm); female: 2 3/4 in (7 cm)* ➤ *77°F (25°C)*
Sociable with large fish not of its own species

Like most African cichlids, this species is very robust and easy to raise. Nonetheless, you should provide this fish with the largest amount of space possible in an aquarium with an elevated pH and a constant temperature. Mussels and small crustaceans are the staple of its diet, which also includes plant life. If you are successful in your efforts at breeding them (which is relatively easy in captivity), you will be able to notice that it is the female who incubates the eggs, which are kept in her mouth for two to three weeks before hatching.

Aequidens curviceps

Flag Cichlid, Sheepshead Acara

➤ *Amazon* ➤ *Male: 3 in (8 cm); female: 2 1/3 in (6 cm)* ➤ *72° to 79°F (22° to 26°C)*
Territorial while breeding

With skin highlighted by olive green reflections speckled with blue, this attractive cichlid has a peaceful temperament. Aquarium plants are essential for its well-being, and at the appropriate moment, they serve as depositing areas for the spawn. All the construction work undertaken while building the nest can expose the plant roots, so it is important to rearrange the decor afterward in accordance with the plants' needs. Breeding is among the most prolific of any fish in captivity, and the parents are very attentive to the needs of their fry.

Haplochromis moorii

Blue Lumphead, Blue Moori

➤ *From Lake Malawi to Lake Malombe* ➤ *9 in (23 cm)*
➤ *77°F (25°C)*
Territorial without being too aggressive

The principal characteristic of this large fish with its magnificent electric blue color resides in the fact that the male, upon attaining adult age, grows a large bump on his head. Lively like most cichlids, it is distinguished from its cousins, such as the *Cichlasoma*, by its great respect for its habitat. In other words, it leaves the plants and other vegetation in the condition in which it found them upon entering the tank. Easy to raise in a large aquarium, it is also easy to breed in captivity. The female is a mouthbreeder–she incubates the eggs in her mouth.

Cichlasoma synspilum

Redheaded Cichlid

➤ *Central America* ➤ *$9\frac{3}{4}$ to $11\frac{2}{3}$ in (25 to 30 cm)* ➤ *79° to 82°F (26° to 28°C)*
Quarrelsome

Measuring 10 in (25 cm) and sometimes more than 12 in (30 cm) for the male and combative by nature, this fish needs a large aquarium. The aquarium should hold anywhere from 150 to 200 gal (600 to 800 L), where each of its fellows—carefully chosen from among different genera (such as *Copora, Thorichthys,* or *Nandopsis*)—will easily find its own niche; otherwise, the serenity of the tank will be troubled. This stocky fish is fierce in combat. In addition, *C. synspilum* care little about maintaining the environment in which they swim, tearing up and nibbling at the vegetation, knocking over rocks and roots.

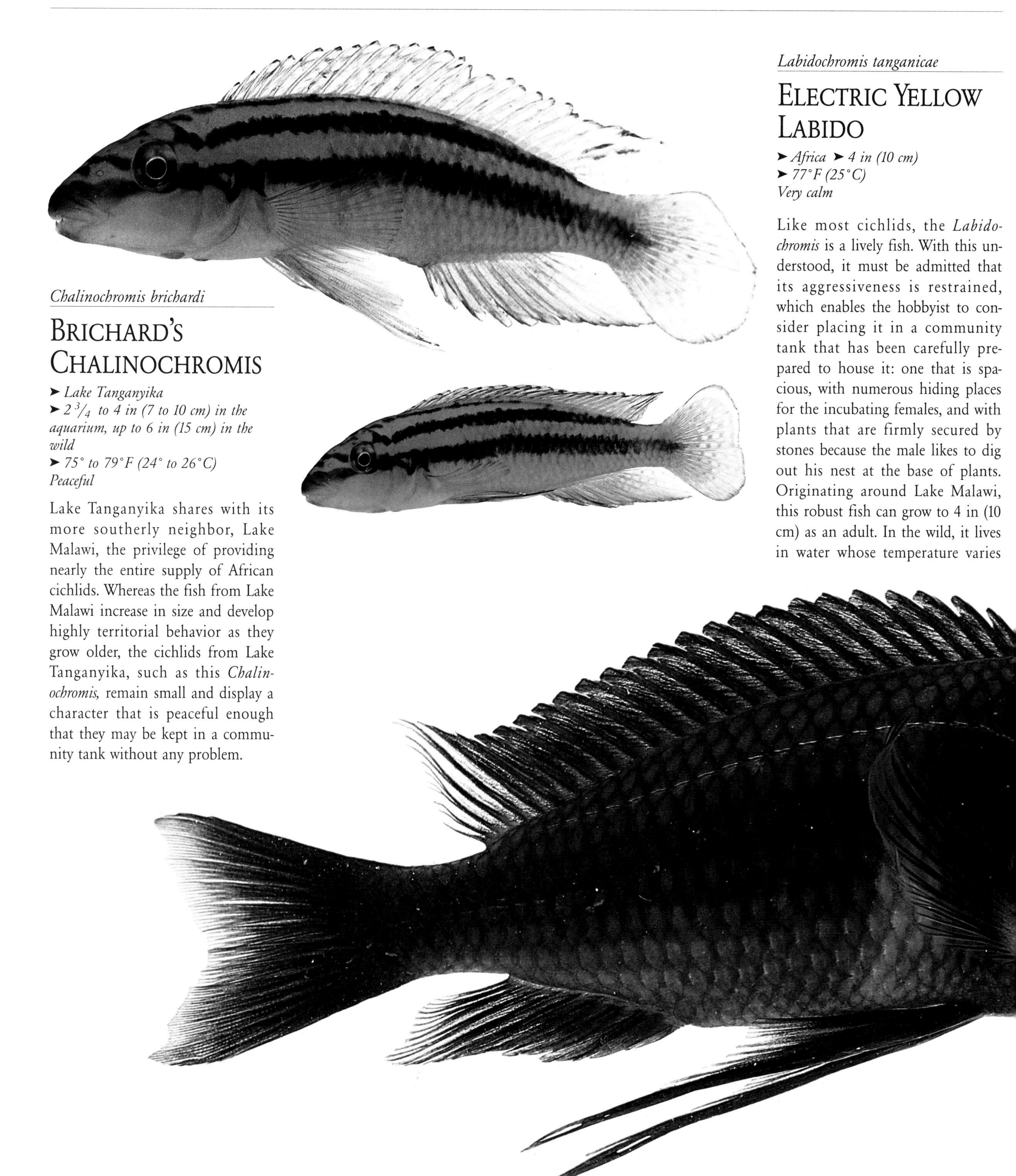

Chalinochromis brichardi

BRICHARD'S CHALINOCHROMIS

➤ *Lake Tanganyika*
➤ *2 3/4 to 4 in (7 to 10 cm) in the aquarium, up to 6 in (15 cm) in the wild*
➤ *75° to 79°F (24° to 26°C)*
Peaceful

Lake Tanganyika shares with its more southerly neighbor, Lake Malawi, the privilege of providing nearly the entire supply of African cichlids. Whereas the fish from Lake Malawi increase in size and develop highly territorial behavior as they grow older, the cichlids from Lake Tanganyika, such as this *Chalinochromis*, remain small and display a character that is peaceful enough that they may be kept in a community tank without any problem.

Labidochromis tanganicae

ELECTRIC YELLOW LABIDO

➤ *Africa* ➤ *4 in (10 cm)*
➤ *77°F (25°C)*
Very calm

Like most cichlids, the *Labidochromis* is a lively fish. With this understood, it must be admitted that its aggressiveness is restrained, which enables the hobbyist to consider placing it in a community tank that has been carefully prepared to house it: one that is spacious, with numerous hiding places for the incubating females, and with plants that are firmly secured by stones because the male likes to dig out his nest at the base of plants. Originating around Lake Malawi, this robust fish can grow to 4 in (10 cm) as an adult. In the wild, it lives in water whose temperature varies

between 77° and 82°F (25° and 28°C). This brightly colored fish is especially interesting because it sports a remarkable lemon-yellow coat that, with age, gradually turns golden yellow, a very rare shade for freshwater fish, and because it has attractive black markings on its dorsal, pelvic, and anal fins.

Tropheus duboisi

DUBOISI, WHITE-SPOTTED CICHLID

➤ *Lake Tanganyika* ➤ *4 to 4 2/3 in (10 to 12 cm)* ➤ *75° to 79°F (24° to 26°C)*
Aggressive

Pictured here is the adult form of an African cichlid that comes from Lake Tanganyika. As the months go by, this fish will, on reaching adulthood, lose the attractive star designs that decorate its flanks. The intensity of its colors will dwindle away, and its charming small white spots will disappear in favor of a more uniform blue and a more ordinary stripe. The water composition of Lake Taganyika is characterized by moderate hardness combined with a rather elevated pH, anywhere from 8.5 to 9. Very territorial and limivorous, this cichlid eats algae, silt, and whatever small prey make their home in the silt. Nonetheless, it is absolutely essential to keep it from red worms. Unable to digest them properly, it is prone to intestinal bloating that may result in death.

Thorichthys meeki

FIREMOUTH

➤ *Guatemala, Yucatán* ➤ *4 to 6 in (10 to 15 cm)*
➤ *72° to 77°F (22° to 25°C)*
Territorial

Breeding in Asian countries has not taken place without fostering some changes in this fish. Its head has become more rectilinear and the original coloration of its neck, an attractive red, has turned orange. Nonetheless, it must be admitted that its appearance has lost none of its beautiful allure in captivity. Its temperament, civil except when breeding, leads the Firemouth to avoid picking quarrels with its tankmates. Although it will not eat the aquarium plants, its concern for securing refuges for itself may lead it, when hollowing out its nest, to lay bare the base of plants to such an extent that the plants are torn from their moorings. When desiring to breed, the environment needs to be properly arranged beforehand: sand, tipped-over pots, and neutral water at 79°F (26°C).

Papiliochromis ramirezi

BLUE RAM

➤ *Venezuela, Colombia*
➤ *2 to 2 3/4 in (5 to 7 cm) for specimens raised in fish farms*
➤ *75° to 79°F (24° to 26°C)*
Agreeable in a group

Neolamprologus leleupi

LEMON CICHLID

➤ *Lake Tanganyika*
➤ *4 in (10 cm)* ➤ *77°F (25°C)*
Territorial, especially when breeding

This is an attractive and very interesting fish whose tapered body (especially the slender head) is perfectly in sync with the rocky environment of its native lake. It threads its way about everywhere and is equally at home both in the crevices of the decor and in the dense plant growth. This means that the period of its adjustment to the aquarium (which must necessarily be quite large) will be marked by a spate of avalanches. Living in couples, these fish lose their peaceful character as soon as the integrity of their territory is at stake. It must be noted that this cichlid has little appetite for dry food and that it prefers small aquatic worms. Breeding is easy and very prolific.

This attractive cichlid can be placed in a community tank with small species. Extremely colorful, it displays the entire spectrum of a luminous prism. True, it never grows very large, but its shyness and peaceful habits make this fish a fine neighbor, even in a tank of modest proportions, for small characids from South America, such as the Cardinal or Neon Tetras. The aquarium should be well planted. Only a strong susceptibility to various illnesses (tuberculosis, white-spot disease) and to abrupt changes in water quality leave it relatively fragile and prevent it from realizing a long life.

Pterophyllum scalare

Gold Angelfish and Black Angelfish

➤ *Amazon basin* ➤ *6 in (15 cm), including fins*
➤ *75° to 82°F (24° to 28°C)*
Calm with large fish

Julidochromis sp.

Julie

➤ *Tanzania* ➤ *2 3/4 in (7 cm)*
➤ *77°F (25°C)*
Territorial, aggressive toward fish with similar markings

This small striped Julie, only 3 in (7 cm), is originally from Lake Tanganyika. Swimming in strongly aerated water at 77°F (25°C), this is a good-natured fish, even if it sometimes displays aggression, which never lasts for very long since the Julie scarcely has the muscle to back up its ambitions. The best way to keep it calm is to provide it with a decor that resembles its natural habitat: plenty of rocks for it to dart around, thereby marking its territory and its spawning grounds.

A very popular and commonly kept aquarium fish, the angelfish today comes exclusively from fish farms in Asia, Eastern Europe, and the southeastern United States. Graceful and robust, it can live for seven or eight years without difficulty, but it requires a rather large tank, at least 40 gal (150 L), and a well-planted environment. If introduced to other fish while still young, it behaves well. On the other hand, in an aquarium that already contains large angelfish, you should only introduce other large fish. Should you try to do otherwise, you will create a *casus belli,* a cause for war. Not picky, the angelfish eats a bit of everything, live or frozen, and so long as it is not from wild stock, it adapts to all kinds of water. Nonetheless, for breeding, which is easy to bring about, angelfish require water with a weak mineral content and a neutral, slightly acid pH. Two possibilities present themselves to the breeder once the female has laid her eggs on a leaf or on some other support. First, one can leave the parents together. In this case, the parents will protect the eggs by chasing away all intruders found circling around the leaf. During this period, the male, who is in charge of the maintenance of the eggs until they hatch, will tolerate the presence even of his companion only with some difficulty since he is kept so busy with cleaning and guarding the eggs. The dietary independence of the fry is assured for forty-eight hours because of the yolk sac. After this they will have to be fed with liquid fry food until they are large enough to accept standard food. But since there is a risk of the parents devouring their first eggs, we recommend the second method, which consists of removing the eggs, along with a bit of water, and placing them in an isolated tank with the male. After forty-eight hours, the fry will hatch and the father should be removed.

From left to right: The Black Angelfish, the Gold Angelfish, and the veil-tailed Zebra Angelfish.

Nimbochromis venustus, Cyrtocara venusta

VENUSTUS

➤ *Lake Malawi* ➤ *8 to 10 in (21 to 26 cm)* ➤ *77°F (25°C)*
Territorial

The colors and markings are even more beautiful in the male, who also is chunkier than the female. This stocky fish needs a large aquarium whose bottom is covered in sand since it likes to hollow out the ground. Plan on a stable rocky decor that includes grottoes where it can hide. This territorial fish can be aggressive toward all fish of similar size and markings. Feasting on meat and plant foods, it also eats flake food. The female Venustus is responsible for incubating the eggs, which she keeps in her mouth before releasing them after absorption of the yolk sac.

Helostomatidae

Lively and dynamic, the fish from the only genus in this family come from Thailand, Malaysia, Borneo, and Sumatra. It is their unique behavior that has made them famous.

Helostoma temminckii

KISSING GOURAMI

➤ *Borneo, Thailand, Sumatra, Malaysia* ➤ *4 to 8 in (10 to 21 cm) in the aquarium, up to 12 in (31 cm) in the wild*
➤ *72° to 82°F (22° to 28°C)*
Sociable, can be aggressive to others of its kind

The Kissing Gourami is so named because of its distinctive puckered lips. This feature has also made it a very popular aquarium fish. However, the "kissing" does not seem to be connected with copulation, instead it is more a show of force. Because of these aggressive tendencies, it is better to keep more than two together in a tank. These fish can live more than ten years in an aquarium, and sometimes even as long as fifteen years. With its strong character, the Kissing Gourami sometimes disturbs calmer species. Breeding has been observed in captivity, but is not especially prolific. Spawning takes place on leaves, not in a nest of bubbles.

Mormyridae

This African family has in its midst a fish that is celebrated in myth, a fish whose brain is proportionally heavier than our own. It has the disadvantage of practically never breeding in captivity; it is, on the other hand, an odd fish that is easy to care for.

Gnathonemus petersii

Elephantnose, Peter's Elephantnose

➤ *Africa* ➤ *7 in (18 cm) in the aquarium, 9 in (23 cm) in the wild*
➤ *77°F (25°C)*
Peaceful but aggressive toward its family if the aquarium is not large enough

This strange fish has many unusual features. Its name is derived from the appendage at the end of its chin, just under its mouth, in the form of a trunk, which it uses to dig around the muddy bottom in search of food. Living in communities in the ponds and rivers of central Africa, the Elephantnose prefers areas that are shady, grassy, and shallow. With a brain that measures more than 3% of its total weight—compared to the human brain which is just 2.3%, and other fish whose brain is less than 1 percent—this fish is extremely intelligent. It analyzes the data transmitted by various nerve centers distributed under its skin. In accordance with the principle of sonar, it gains information about the position of obstacles and prey with the aid of electric sensors located on its caudal peduncle. Consequently, since it is equipped in this fashion, it can compensate for very poor vision, which is caused by a membrane covering its eyes, probably in order to protect the Elephantnose while it is digging about. In the aquarium, it grows to 7 in (18 cm) and requires dimly lit water with a slightly acid pH. Strict in its diet, it eats mainly live worms and other small invertebrates, but will accept frozen food from time to time.

Because of its interesting features, this fish has had many myths and legends associated with it. Venerated by artists from the earliest Egyptian antiquity, it was painted and carved on a large number of tombs. One very popular legend concerns the death of the Egyptian god Osiris. Seth, his brother, killed him after an argument and threw the pieces of the body into the Nile. Disconsolate but determined, Osiris's widow, Isis, recovered the corpse and attempted to restore it to its original form, but was missing one piece: The phallus had disappeared, swallowed by the ancestor of the Elephantnose. This fish then assumed the shape of the missing part.

Mastacembelidae

This family with relatively few members groups together large serpentine fish that are active at night. They inhabit fresh and brackish waters in Southeast Asia and in tropical Africa.

Mastacembelus erythrotaenia

FIRE EEL, SPOTTED FIRE EEL

➤ *Southeast Asia* ➤ *Up to 39 in (1 m)* ➤ *75° to 82°F (24° to 28°C)*
Aggressive toward its own species

This very large fish is best adopted at as early an age as possible. It should be placed in a large tank with a sandy bottom and plenty of rocks and plants where it can conceal itself. Hiding during the day, it is very active at night. Over time, its life in the community tank can gradually become peaceful, and the Fire Eel can come to take scraps from the hand of its owner, even lifting its head out of the water in order to search for the food. Earthworms, *Tubifex* worms, and other live food should be offered frequently. If well fed, the Fire Eel is less likely to eat its smaller tankmates.

Polypteridae

These nocturnally active predators absorb air at the water's surface. They are found throughout tropical Africa.

Erpetoichthys calabaricus

Ropefish, Snakefish

➤ *Tropical Africa* ➤ *14 to 16 in (36 to 41 cm)* ➤ *72° to 82°F (22° to 28°C)*
Predatory

Despite its serpentine body and the absence of any pelvic fins, this aquatic animal has been classified as a fish. The ropefish hides amid the rocks and plants during the day, and it hunts its prey at night. This sly predator hardly gives a chance to whatever fish passes within reach of its teeth. In addition to fish, the ropefish accepts earthworms and other invertebrates.

Tetraodontidae

These large, squat fish with protruding eyes have the odd feature of being able to inflate themselves so that they may be carried by the current.

Tetraodon fluviatilis

Green Puffer

➤ *Southeast Asia* ➤ *2 3/4 in (7 cm) in the aquarium, 4 2/3 to 6 in (12 to 15 cm) in the wild* ➤ *73° to 77°F (23° to 25°C) Best kept by itself, especially as an adult*

This is one of the rare representatives of this family that lives in both freshwater and brackish water. This curious, scaleless fish has pockets in its entrails that it can inflate with water when it wants, just like ballast. This feature enables the puffer to float effortlessly during high tide, borne by the current alone, without rolling or pitching. Its mouth is furnished with a beak, which is very useful when the fish eats all the small snails lying about in the aquarium, but dangerous when this tool becomes a weapon used against other fish. This somewhat aggressive fish requires vigilance. It eats live or frozen food.

Toxotidae

Represented only by the archerfish of the genus Toxotes, *the Toxotidae, originally from Asia and northern Australia, enjoy brackish water. This does not stop them from having a keen eye when it is a matter of capturing their prey by means of an extremely precise spray of water.*

Toxotes jaculatrix

ARCHERFISH

➤ *Southeast Asia, Australia* ➤ *6 in (15 cm) in the aquarium, 8 to 10 in (21 to 26 cm) in the wild*
➤ *77° to 86°F (25° to 30°C)*
Strong with the weak, weak with the strong

The archerfish is a specialized hunter. Equipped with powerful muscles, it projects a spray of water against its victims so strong and precise that even at a distance of 5 ft (1.5 m) it throws off balance and knocks down those unfortunate enough to hover over its hunting ground. To take full advantage of this fish's unusual feature, it is a good idea to leave it in a special large-sized tank, 80 gal (300 L) minimum, knowing that it is impossible for the archerfish to live with others unless they are of the same size. In fact, the ideal environment in which to show off the archerfish to its full advantage is the aqua-terrarium. The aqua-terrarium includes a large surface area without an alkaline pH, with a supplement of salt—these are the ingredients that will help maintain it in top form. Of course, it is also essential that it be fed only live prey.

Scatophagidae

These large fish have the reputation of swallowing everything in sight. In reality, they are exceptionally beneficial since they conveniently clear the bottom of the aquarium of all the animal and vegetable waste products that gather there.

Scatophagus argus, subsp. *atromaculatus (*sold under the name *Scatophagus* "Rubrifons"*)*

RED SCAT, RUBY SCAT

➤ *East India and neighboring islands* ➤ *6 in (15 cm) in the aquarium, 12 in (31 cm) in the wild* ➤ *68° to 82°F (20° to 28°C)*
Peaceful

As its Latin name indicates, the *Scatophagus* is not very particular about the quality of its food. If you do not keep an eye on it, this omnivorous fish will eat anything and everything, alive or dead, passing within its range. It also grazes on aquarium plants. This is a large fish, which despite its best efforts cannot digest all that it eats. Therefore, the clarity of its water is exceptionally compromised; its waste products must be eliminated by very powerful filters.

It must also be noted that even if this magnificent fish prefers to swim in fresh or brackish waters during its youth, the adults will have to be moved to a saltwater tank in order to find their natural habitat.

Saltwater Fish

Holocentridae

The Holocentridae *are divided into two subfamilies: squirrelfish and soldierfish. During the day they live in grottoes since they are primarily nocturnal creatures. It is at night that they search for their food, which consists of invertebrates and small fish. Most live in schools, but others do live by themselves or in couples. Although very active, they are not aggressive toward their own kind or other species. However, do avoid keeping them with small fish.*

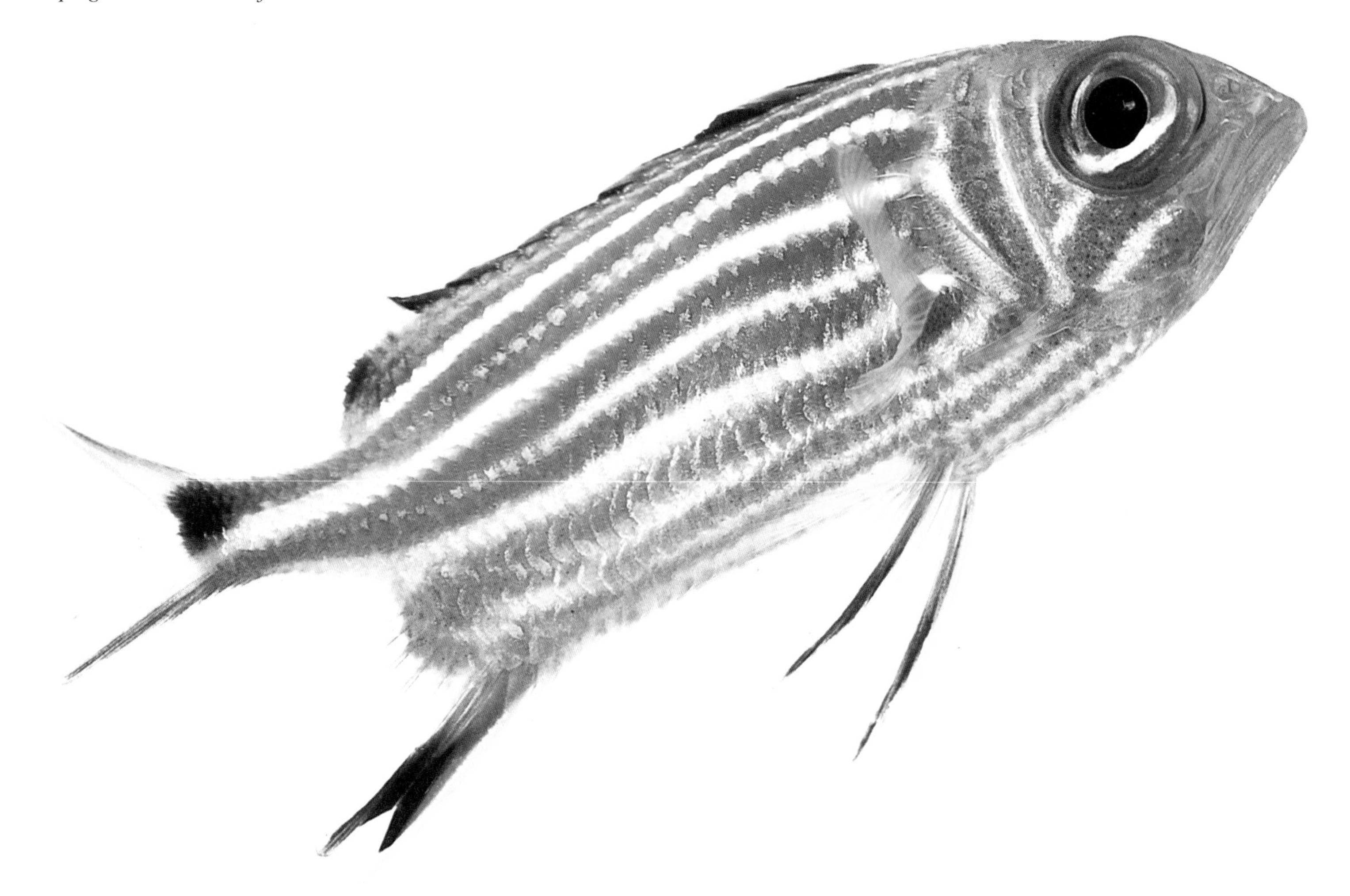

Holocentrus sp.

SQUIRRELFISH

➤ *Tropical seas* ➤ *6 to 10 in (15 to 26 cm)* ➤ *77°F (25°C) on average*
Not to be placed in a community tank

The squirrelfish owes its name to the similarity of its coat to that of certain North American squirrels. Its large eyes are probably the result of having to adapt to a nocturnal lifestyle. A fierce nighttime hunter, it eats anything that moves. This excellent swimmer leaves little hope for its prey. It is advisable not to introduce the squirrelfish to a community tank. First giving it alevin helps it adapt to its home and eventually get used to small live prey or frozen food for its supper.

Muraenidae

The well-developed musculature of the morays and their strong set of teeth, have contributed a great deal to the establishment of their more or less legendary reputation. They live hidden under stones or in hollows during the day, and their principal activity, hunting, is mostly performed at night. These fish are actually not very aggressive and attack only as a defense, at which point their bites are rarely benign. They may be easily maintained in captivity since they are insensitive to the composition of the water and they can eat almost anything. On the other hand, it is essential to provide some hiding places, preferably solid ones, since morays are strong fish. Avoid placing them with small fish at any cost; only the Balistidae and the boxfishes incur no threat from them.

Gymnothorax favagineus

Reticulated Moray Eel, Honeycomb Moray

➤ *Red Sea, Indo-Pacific region*
➤ *4 ft (1.2 m)* ➤ *77°F (25°C)*
Peaceful with its own kind, should be placed only with large fish such as the Balistidae

Easily cared for, the moray spends most of its time in a hiding place from which it does not exit except to hunt. In captivity, it is easily tamed and will not hesitate to eat from the hand of its owner. Such familiarity, however, is not recommended, for its vision is far from excellent and its bite is in fact very painful, since its teeth are tilted toward the back of the throat in order to prevent its prey from escaping. It accepts all food of animal origin. Its life span appears to be quite long: over six years.

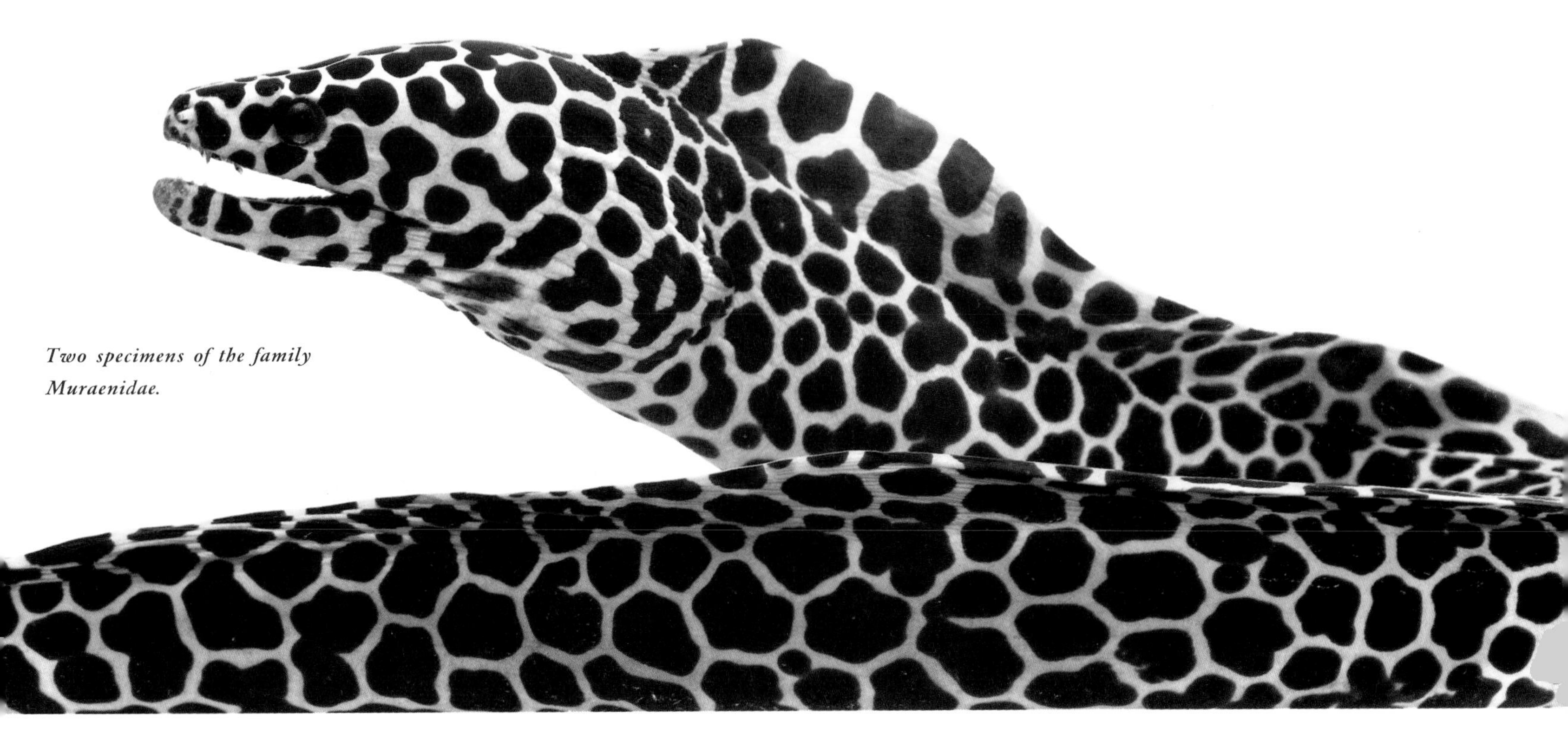

Two specimens of the family Muraenidae.

Syngnathidae

Deprived of scales, the small number of fish in this family also lack teeth and have no gill covers. They are also poor swimmers. But their prehensile tails, which lack caudal fins, compensate for these shortcomings. The grace of their gently undulating movements is more than enough to win the sea horse appreciation. Responding only to moving prey, these fish are obliged to dilate their mouths to swallow their food. If they are ill at ease in a community tank, include some invertebrates. Their life span barely exceeds four years, and is on average much shorter in the aquarium.

Hippocampus sp.

Sea Horse

➤ *Indo-Pacific region* ➤ *4 to 12 in (10 to 31 cm)* ➤ *77°F (25°C)*
Shy and very timid

The bizarre and primitive appearance of the sea horse continually fascinates the observer. Relatively inactive, it does not require a large aquarium. Be sure to provide it with a carefully laid-out interior with supports and plants to which it can anchor itself. It is best to keep it in the company of invertebrates, except for anemones and *Cerianthus*.

Its mating customs are unusual. The innovative aspect of its mating habits is the fact that it is the female who introduces her ovipositor (spawning tube) into the belly pouch of the male. After fertilization of the eggs, the incubation period takes roughly eighteen days for tropical species. After mating, the female returns to her daily activities, while the male endures a solitary delivery that generally takes several days. The sea horse usually feeds on *Mysis*, alevins, and live or frozen daphnia.

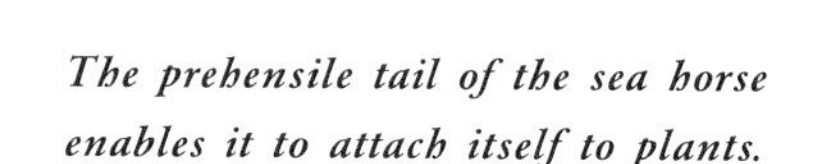

The prehensile tail of the sea horse enables it to attach itself to plants.

Scorpaenidae

The family Scorpaenidae includes fish whose heads are completely or partially covered with bony plates studded with poisonous quills, giving them the appearance of hedgehogs. Normally bottom dwellers, they lie hidden and camouflaged as they hunt from a stationary post. In the aquarium, they easily feed on prey that venture to the bottom. They suffer, however, if there is any competition for food. In addition, avoid being stung by the poisonous rays of their fins, which cause sharp pains that can be alleviated only by applying very hot water.

Pterois sp.

LIONFISH

➤ *Pacific Ocean* ➤ *12 in (31 cm)* ➤ *77°F (25°C)*
Peaceful with large fish

This attractive and very robust fish would be unhappy in any aquarium smaller than 80 g (300 L). As long as this condition is met, it will gracefully swim about, majestically unfurling its undulating fins. However, the quills at the ends of the rays of this peaceful beauty's dorsal fin are connected to a pouch containing a poison that is similar to that of the cobra. Thus, even if its natural placidity never leads the lionfish to attack, it is strongly advised that you not risk handling this fish at all, since its sting is extremely painful. Peaceful with those that are too large for it to swallow, this fish accepts only live food at first. Its mouth is so enormous that it simply inhales food without even chewing it.

Grammidae

This family includes some nine species from the Atlantic Ocean, the Caribbean, and eastern Australia. These calm fish are small in size, strongly colored, and have several hard rays on their fins. Maintenance is easy, as long as there is no competition for their food and they are provided with shelters where they can hide.

Gramma loreto

Royal Gramma

➤ *Bermuda, Caribbean islands, the Bahamas* ➤ *3 in (8 cm)*
➤ *77°F (25°C)*
Peaceful and timid

The Royal Gramma is colored in a pretty shade of violet at the anterior end, which blends into a delicate nuance of orangish-pink at the posterior. It is a regular visitor to coral reefs, for it is here that this timid creature can hide from related species, with which it does not get along. It is comfortable in a tank containing invertebrates, which it respects, and calm fish, which respect it and leave its food alone. It adapts easily to the tank if you feed it small live prey.

Plesiopidae

Constituting a small family of only nine species, the Plesiopidae spend most of their time hidden in the crevices of coral reefs. Calm and fearful, they are active only after nightfall. The presence of overly active fish nearby can unsettle them. Their life span is short: hardly four years in an aquarium.

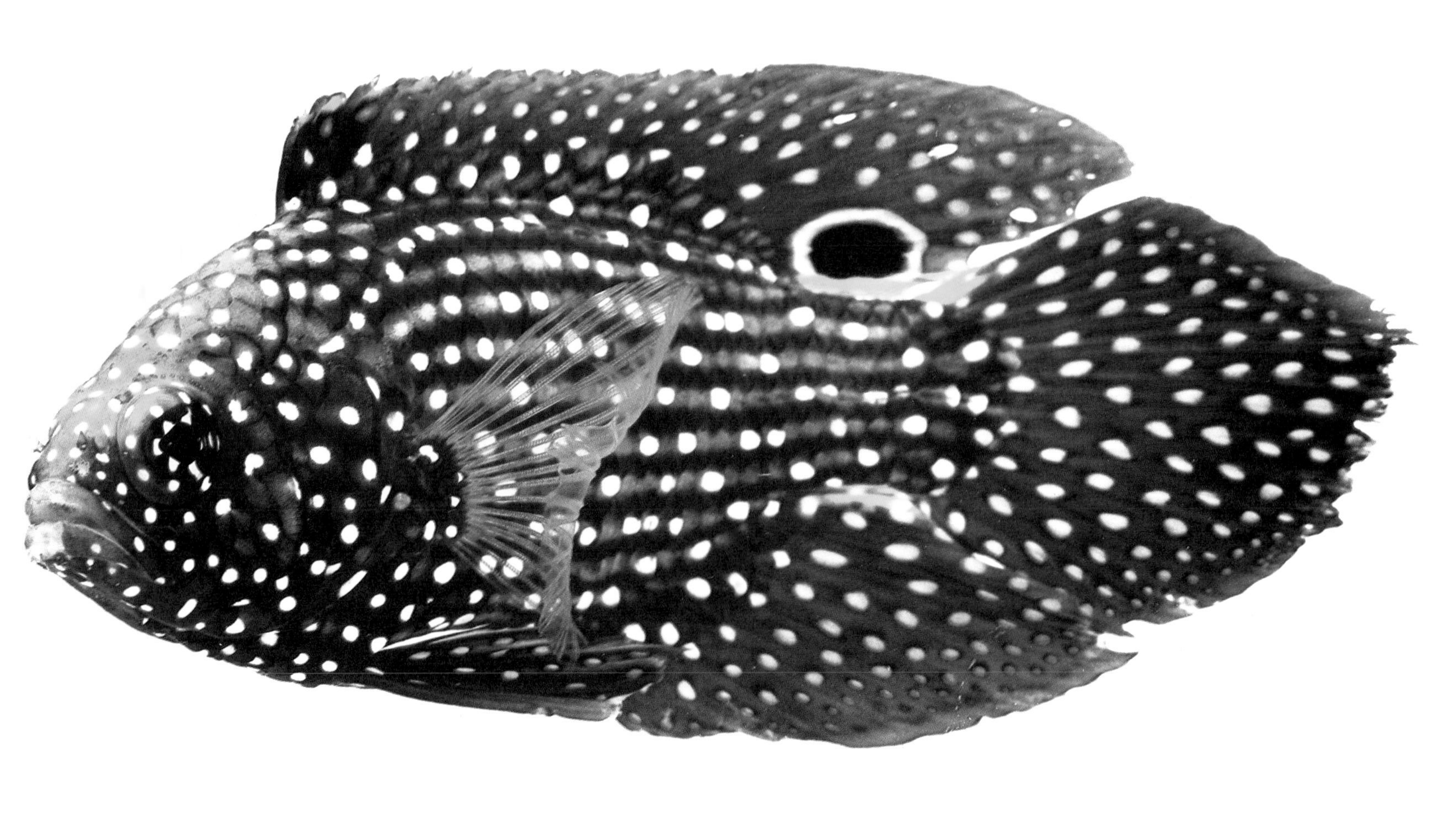

Calloplesiops altivelis

COMET, MARINE BETTA

➤ *Indo-Pacific region* ➤ *6 to 7 in (15 to 18 cm)* ➤ *75° to 79°F (24° to 26°C)*
Solitary and timid

With its large fine fins, speckled with a thousand brilliant white points like a nighttime sky, and with its trademark black ocellus ringed with white on its dorsal fin, the Marine Betta is majestically impressive. Famed for its abilities as a fighter, this splendid fish is a recluse cloaked in veils. Because of its extreme timidity, it cannot tolerate the presence of any of its related species, but it is easily kept in the company of calm fish and large invertebrates. It lives in constant hiding amid the cracks and crevices of the aquarium decor, and shows itself only after nightfall. In other words, it is so discreet that you are hardly ever afforded the chance to enjoy even a glimpse of it. During the day, if it feels at all healthy, it hides; should it show its face, then you may conclude that it will soon die. It does not adapt easily to the aquarium. At first, it will accept only small crustaceans or small fish (like guppies) as food. Once the Marine Betta is fully used to the tank, its life expectancy nonetheless proves to be all too brief: less than four years.

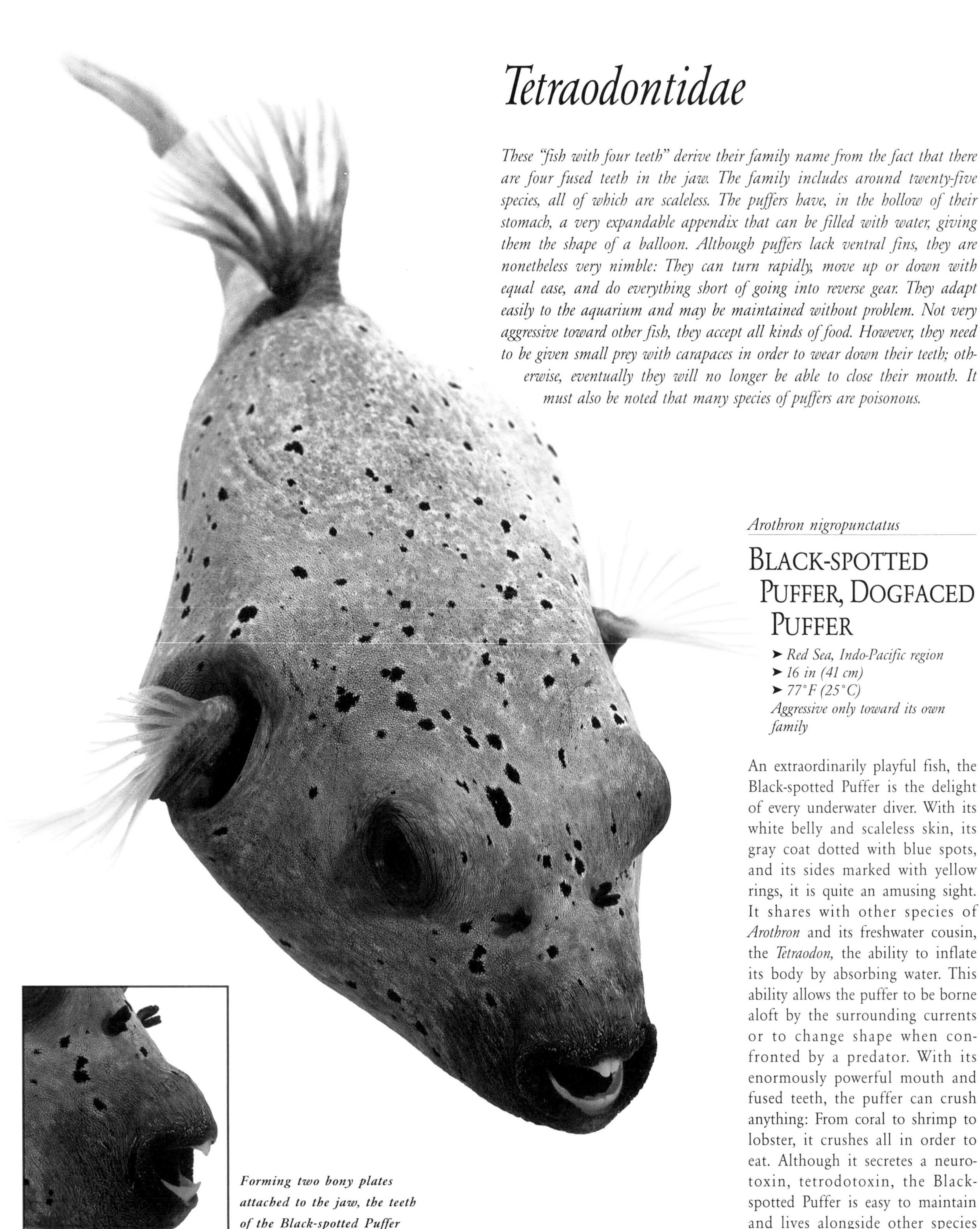

Tetraodontidae

These "fish with four teeth" derive their family name from the fact that there are four fused teeth in the jaw. The family includes around twenty-five species, all of which are scaleless. The puffers have, in the hollow of their stomach, a very expandable appendix that can be filled with water, giving them the shape of a balloon. Although puffers lack ventral fins, they are nonetheless very nimble: They can turn rapidly, move up or down with equal ease, and do everything short of going into reverse gear. They adapt easily to the aquarium and may be maintained without problem. Not very aggressive toward other fish, they accept all kinds of food. However, they need to be given small prey with carapaces in order to wear down their teeth; otherwise, eventually they will no longer be able to close their mouth. It must also be noted that many species of puffers are poisonous.

Arothron nigropunctatus

Black-spotted Puffer, Dogfaced Puffer

- ➤ *Red Sea, Indo-Pacific region*
- ➤ *16 in (41 cm)*
- ➤ *77°F (25°C)*

Aggressive only toward its own family

An extraordinarily playful fish, the Black-spotted Puffer is the delight of every underwater diver. With its white belly and scaleless skin, its gray coat dotted with blue spots, and its sides marked with yellow rings, it is quite an amusing sight. It shares with other species of *Arothron* and its freshwater cousin, the *Tetraodon,* the ability to inflate its body by absorbing water. This ability allows the puffer to be borne aloft by the surrounding currents or to change shape when confronted by a predator. With its enormously powerful mouth and fused teeth, the puffer can crush anything: From coral to shrimp to lobster, it crushes all in order to eat. Although it secretes a neurotoxin, tetrodotoxin, the Black-spotted Puffer is easy to maintain and lives alongside other species without difficulty.

Forming two bony plates attached to the jaw, the teeth of the Black-spotted Puffer enable it to crush its food.

Chaetodontidae

Found in tropical seas, where they swim among the coral reefs, the Chaetodontidae live in couples or remain solitary. All members of the family have a black ocellus near the tail, almost symmetrical to the eye. This eyespot does not fail to surprise potential predators, who are obviously perplexed as to the direction in which their prey will move. Adaptation of butterflyfish in captivity always proves difficult because of their specific dietary requirements and their extreme sensitivity to the water composition. Nonetheless, in an aquarium that is abundantly furnished with algae and hiding places, and in the company of other light eaters, they may live for several years.

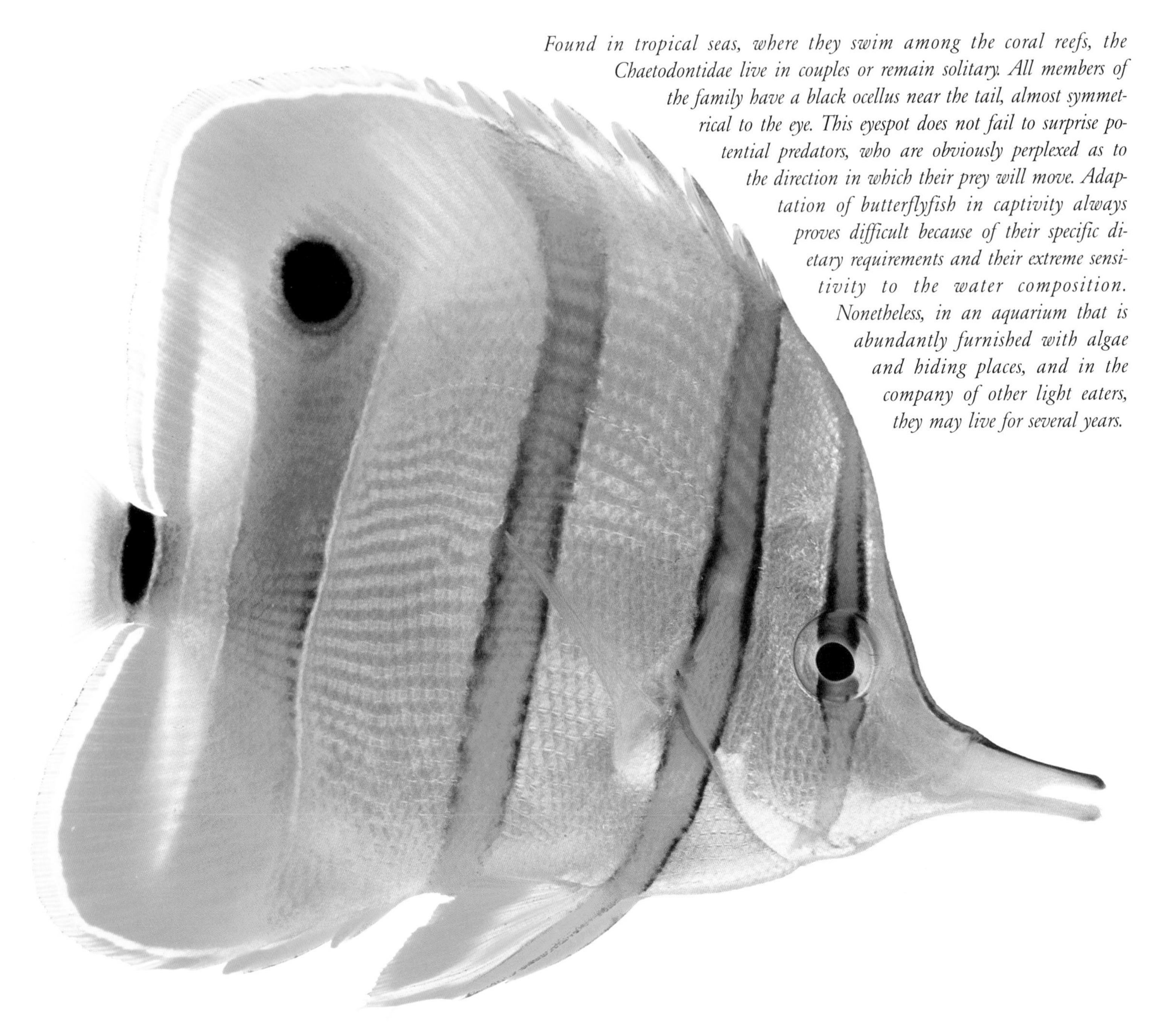

Chelmon rostratus

Copper-banded Butterflyfish, Longnose Butterflyfish

- *Indo-Pacific region*
- *5 to 7 3/4 in (13 to 20 cm)*
- *79°F (26°C)*

Peaceful toward other species

If you are not careful, it is easy to confuse the black ocellus near the top of this fish's dorsal fin with its eye, located low down at the opposite end. In all probability, the Copper-banded Butterflyfish uses this illusion to confuse predators. This trickery is the perfect example of *trompe l'oeil.* The odd snout, which resembles the beak of a wading bird, enables the fish to dig around in sand and coral. Difficult to keep even in a large aquarium, this butterflyfish prefers to live in a school. It feeds on live crustaceans, and after a period of adaptation, it will accept substitute foods. Since it has a light appetite, avoid placing it with more voracious eaters, which will invariably ruin your chances of seeing it feed.

Chaetodon auriga

THREADFIN BUTTERFLYFISH, GOLDEN BUTTERFLYFISH, AURIGA BUTTERFLYFISH

➤ *Indo-Pacific region (*C. auriga setifer, *with a black ocellus on the dorsal fin), Red Sea (*C. a. auriga, *with no ocellus on the dorsal fin)* ➤ *5 to 8 in (13 to 21 cm)* ➤ *79°F (26°C)*
Aggressive toward its own family but peaceful toward others

Chaetodon lunula

RACCOON BUTTERFLYFISH

➤ *Red Sea, Indo-Pacific region* ➤ *7 to 7 3/4 in (18 to 20 cm)* ➤ *77°F (25°C)*
Aggressive toward its own family but peaceful toward others

The Raccoon Butterflyfish is marvelously decorated in an unusual pattern in various shades of yellow, black, and white. Along with the *C. auriga*, the *C. collare*, and the *C. vagabundus*, it is one of the hardiest of the Chaetodontidae, which include many genera and species. Unfortunately, most are difficult to maintain in captivity since they do not readily accept food substitution. Avoid introducing this *Chaetodon* (as well as any of the other genera) to an aquarium containing invertebrates as the butterflyfish will eat them all.

The Threadfin Butterflyfish is slightly more hardy than the Copper-banded Butterflyfish. In a large tank, it never stops moving, drawing attention to the magnificent nuances of its coloring, a potpourri of yellow, white, and black. It is prone to attack fish that are similarly colored, relying on its snout, which in calmer moments it uses to rummage about in search of shrimp and algae. Above all, do not place it with invertebrates.

Forcipiger flavissimus

Yellow Longnose Butterflyfish

➤ Red Sea, Indo-Pacific region ➤ 7 to 10 in (18 to 26 cm) ➤ 77°F (25°C)
Peaceful in a large aquarium, aggressive toward its own species in a small tank

Clearly this fish has an appreciably longer snout than the *Chelmon rostratus,* and thus a greater ability to rummage about. Like its cousin, it has a black ocellus at its tail end, but whereas the *C. rostratus* has its ocellus on the dorsal fin, that on this fish is at the back of the anal fin. The Yellow Longnose Butterflyfish is rather difficult to maintain. The best results are obtained by starting off with very healthy subjects, ones that are not noticeably thin, and giving them small live prey, *Artemia, Mysis*, cyclops, and daphnia. Another species, *F. longirostris,* is similar in appearance, except that its snout is even longer. Both species are difficult to find commercially.

Pomacanthidae

Most fish in this family change color as they mature. All species are beautiful. Angelfish live as recluses, even as couples. They are territorial and very aggressive, and their adaptability is iffy because of their dietary requirements.

The young Emperor Angelfish has a blue coat with a row of concentric white rings, a pattern that changes with age.

Pomacanthus imperator

EMPEROR ANGELFISH

➤ *Red Sea, Indo-Pacific region* ➤ *10 to 15 in (26 to 38 cm)* ➤ *77°F (25°C)*
Aggressive toward its tankmates, especially its own family

In its juvenile form, the Emperor Angelfish displays coloration that is clearly different from what will later be its adult markings. When young, it is blue with white stripes, and the back of its body is decorated with concentric white circles. As it ages, the fish turns a nice blue-green shade, and the white stripes give way to lines of a beautiful yellow, the same color as its caudal fin. This photogenic fish adapts well to the aquarium, especially if it is introduced while still young. In order to facilitate its acclimation, feed it often with small live prey to which you can gradually add finely chopped plants, spinach, and small pieces of cooked algae. Because it dines at a leisurely pace on whatever dish it is served, avoid placing it with voracious eaters. The Emperor Angelfish is not very sociable and is even occasionally aggressive.

Centropyge bispinosus

CORAL BEAUTY

➤ *Indo-Pacific region as far as Australia* ➤ *3 in (8 cm) in the aquarium, 5 in (13 cm) in the wild* ➤ *77°F (25°C)*
Aggressive toward its family

The Coral Beauty dislikes competition and will readily kill a more attractive rival, especially when mating. Territorial defense constitutes its principal activity. This species is easily maintained, feeding happily on pieces of lettuce, spinach, small crustaceans, and other live foods. For long-term success, the main portion of the diet should be vegetable matter.

Arusetta asfur

PURPLE MOON ANGELFISH, ARABIAN ANGELFISH

➤ *Red Sea* ➤ *8 in (21 cm) in the aquarium, 14 in (36 cm) in the wild* ➤ *77°F (25°C)*
Timid

This fish exhibits characteristics similar to those of its cousin the Emperor Angelfish, except that it is more difficult to maintain. To help even the odds, you must purchase the Purple Moon Angelfish while still young, place it in a very large tank provided with nooks, in which it enjoys hiding, and above all guard against abrupt changes in temperature, which it cannot tolerate. This timid fish spends much of its time in hiding, but when it shows itself, the splendid colors adorning its coat burst forth in all their beauty.

Pygoplites diacanthus

Regal Angelfish

➤ *Red Sea, Indo-Pacific region* ➤ *7 3/4 to 12 in (20 to 31 cm)*
➤ *75° to 77°F (24° to 25°C)*
Timid

The Regal Angelfish is magnificently colored, having a yellow coat striped with blue and white bands. This shy fish does not get along well with members of its family but seems to tolerate other fish. Its Achilles' heel, which explains the difficulty of keeping this fish, is its dietary regimen: It feeds mainly on live sponges, which are very expensive and difficult to find. Nonetheless, with time one can get the Regal Angelfish to accept live *Artemia.* In general, this is not a fish for the home aquarium.

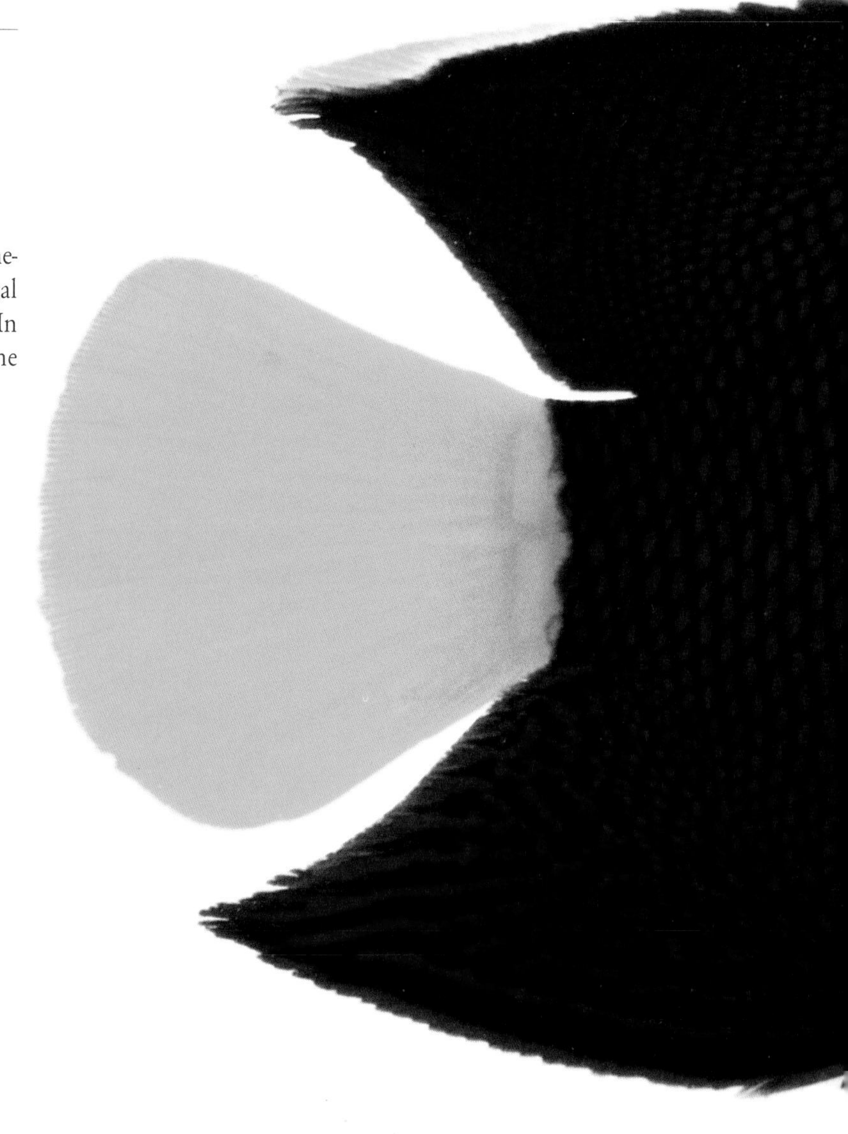

Centropyge loriculus

Flame Angelfish

➤ *Philippines, Hawaiian and Marshall islands* ➤ *$2\frac{3}{4}$ in (7 cm) in the aquarium, $4\frac{2}{3}$ in (12 cm) in the wild* ➤ *77°F (25°C)*
Aggressive toward its own species; peaceful toward others

Unlike the markings of many other species of marine angelfish, the Flame Angelfish's markings do not change with age. This species is easy to maintain, as long as you take care not to place it with members of its own family, with which it has territorial disputes. With others, it gets along well, especially if they are fundamentally different. This fish requires small live prey that have been raised on a diet of algae, but it is not a very voracious eater. It is therefore a good idea to avoid all competition for food by placing it with other light eaters.

Centropyge bicolor

Bicolor Angelfish

➤ *Indo-Pacific region* ➤ *4 to 6 in (10 to 15 cm)* ➤ *77°F (25°C)*
Intolerant of its family

The Bicolor Angelfish is as beautiful as a painting. A yellow fore end and tail, a blue posterior, and a blue band on the head–here is a design that is entirely contemporary. However, the acclimation of this very delicate fish is difficult. Only young subjects have any chance of being acclimated, as long as you take care to give them small prey at first, then a conventional diet accompanied by plants. The Bicolor Angelfish is not a fish for the beginner.

Pomacentridae

More than two hundred species are included in this family of generally small, lively, and highly colorful fish, most of which adapt readily in captivity. The best known of these fish, the damselfish and the clownfish, are found throughout the world. All of them feed principally on invertebrates. When mating, it is usually the male who chooses and cleans the spawning area, and it is always the male who looks after the eggs, fanning them with his pectoral fins and removing those that become infected by fungus. Nonetheless, breeding in captivity is only occasionally successful.

Dascyllus trimaculatus

DOMINO DAMSELFISH

- *Red Sea, Indo-Pacific region*
- *4 to 4 $^{2}/_{3}$ in (10 to 12 cm)*
- *77° to 79°F (25° to 26°C)*

Somewhat aggressive

This fish is an excellent choice for beginners, for its state of health is an index of the health of the whole aquarium. Should the fish die, aquarists would have to conclude that no living creature would be able to stay alive in the tank. The Domino Damselfish is as black as a widow, but when young its appearance of perpetual mourning is lightened by three white spots, one on the face and one on each side of the back. It can become territorial as it matures, venting its hostility on its more timid tankmates. In the wild this fish enjoys shrimp and crab larvae, and feeds where the waters are rich in these creatures, diving as much as 130 ft (40 m) when necessary.

Pomacentrus caeruleus

Electric Blue Damselfish, Blue Devil

➤ Indonesia ➤ 2 1/3 to 3 in (6 to 8 cm) ➤ 77°F (25°C)
Gregarious in the wild, aggressive toward its own species in the aquarium despite its desire to live in a school

The Electric Blue Damselfish is magnificently colored. A quarrelsome fish, it nips at others, especially other damselfish. Toward different species, though, it displays a studied indifference. This fish is a robust swimmer when the water has an elevated pH. It is also easy to feed: Small crustaceans native to its coral home as well as small worms suffice, along with chopped plants. Do not place it in an aquarium with invertebrates.

Amphiprion ocellaris

Common Clownfish

➤ *Indo-Pacific and Indo-Australian regions* ➤ *3 to $4\frac{2}{3}$ in (8 to 12 cm)*
➤ *79°F (26°C)*
Males are occasionally aggressive

This fish exhibits striking coloration. Its body is an intense orange with white bands outlined in black, and its rounded pectoral fins are tipped with black. Like all other species of *Amphiprion*, the Common Clownfish lives in the shelter of various sea anemones. These host invertebrates provide the guest fish with lodging, but do not paralyze the fish with their tentacles or swallow them through their oral opening. Moreover, it is within the shadow of the anemone that two breeding clownfish will build their nest, for the anemone ensures the finest protection against all predatory attempts on the eggs. This fish is difficult to raise in captivity. Although mating may take place without any special difficulty, the feeding of the young is very often problematic for the hobbyist, for they can swallow only microorganisms.

Highly prized because of its beautiful colors, the Common Clownfish is, however, difficult to raise in captivity.

Amphiprion frenatus

TOMATO CLOWNFISH

➤ *Indo-Pacific region, South Africa, Australia* ➤ *3 to 5 in (8 to 13 cm)*
➤ *77° to 79°F (25° to 26°C)*
Aggressive in a small aquarium

This fish has been dubbed a clown, even though the brown of its habit and the white of the collar surrounding its head somewhat suggest a bearded Capuchin monk, an altogether different character. The Tomato Clownfish adapts quickly, as long as you make sure to raise it in a good-sized tank (otherwise the couples attack each other) with an elevated pH and a temperature of 79°F (26°C). Fond of small worms and mussels, it also accepts small crustaceans as food.

Amphiprion clarkii

Clark's Clownfish, Yellow-tailed Clownfish

➤ *Indo-Pacific region*
➤ *4 to 4 2/3 in (10 to 12 cm)*
➤ *77°F (25°C)*
Peaceful

The white band that borders the entire face gives the appearance that this fish has a toothache, while a second band wrapped around its middle looks somewhat like a truss for a hernia. In spite of this costume, accessorized with luminous yellow fins, Clark's Clownfish is nonetheless hardy. A peaceful fish, it swims most contentedly among invertebrates, especially anemones, with which it lives as a guest. In addition, this funny-looking creature is one of the easiest clownfish to acclimate to the aquarium, and so may be recommended to beginning fish hobbyists.

Labridae

This family of six hundred species includes some excellent swimmers who require a lot of space and many hiding places, for they are very independent. Given to digging about in everything, wrasses favor a division of labor: Some prefer oxygenating the sandy bottom of the aquarium; others, cleaning the teeth of large fish. All need sand, whether to hide in at night or in case of danger. If not adequately fed with crustaceans, worms, and aquatic plants, wrasses will supplement their diet with the fins of smaller fish.

Novaculichthys taeniurus

Dragon Wrasse

➤ *Indo-Pacific region* ➤ *7 to $10\frac{1}{2}$ in (18 to 27 cm)* ➤ *77°F (25°C)*
Aggressive toward its own species in a small tank

The Dragon Wrasse has taken its cue from the chameleon, borrowing that creature's highly developed skill of mimicry to provide itself with an iron-clad guarantee of nonaggression on the part of its tankmates, which are commonly irritated by the sight of other fish with intensely colored markings. Indeed, it has developed this skill to the point that young Dragon Wrasses, in a tank rich in algae, very often escape the watchful eye of the aquarist unacquainted with their camouflage skills. Besides using mimicry, they also hide in the sand in case of danger. Be sure therefore to provide a base of fine sand in the aquarium, where even in peacetime the Dragon Wrasses, both juvenile and adult, can spend their nights. Easily maintained if introduced to the tank when young, this fish feeds on crustaceans, small sea urchins, and mollusks. In a small tank, it is rather aggressive toward its own species yet ignores other fish.

In its juvenile form, the Coris formosa *has brown-orange markings and several triangular white spots.*

Coris frerei (previously *C. formosa*)

SADDLEBACK WRASSE, QUEEN WRASSE

➤ *Indo-Pacific region*
➤ *8 in (21 cm) in the aquarium, 19 1/2 to 23 in (50 to 59 cm) in the wild*
➤ *77°F (25°C)*
Sociable when young

The adult and juvenile forms do not much look alike. Also, the young of this and another species, *C. gaimardi,* are so similar that it is difficult to tell them apart unless you know the identification of the parents. Easily raised if introduced to the tank at an early age, they have attractive, mostly red, markings and live relatively calmly in schools. As they mature, they change color, assuming a darker shade. They also become more solitary, and prove to be very aggressive both toward their own species and other fish. Therefore, they require a great deal of space in the aquarium. They are undemanding when it comes to their food, contenting themselves with live prey or dead, which they search for on the sandy bottom. It is there, too, that they often hide.

Labroides dimidiatus

Cleaner Wrasse, Blue Streak

➤ *Indo-Pacific region, Red Sea* ➤ *4 to 4 $^2/_3$ in (10 to 12 cm)* ➤ *79°F (26°C)*
Helpful

The Cleaner Wrasse, with its small, compact body, can be seen in the wild entering the maw of a grouper, cleaning the much larger fish's teeth and picnicking on all the food particles that can be found there. When finished, waste often leaves through the gill slits rather than the mouth. These removers of parasites are organized in "cleaning stations," like clinics, where the numerous "patients" must wait a long time for their turn. Despite the vulnerable position of the Cleaner Wrasses, the much larger fish do not attack them because of the beneficial service they provide. However, they must fear the competition of another fish, the *Aspidontus taeniatus*, which looks like them but does not perform the same service. Taking advantage of the instinctive confidence of their patients, these look-alikes profit by snatching several bites of flesh.

In captivity, the Cleaner Wrasse is difficult to maintain and very often becomes emaciated. The probable reason is that in the aquarium the social hierarchy resumes its basic form: The small fish become vulnerable when up against the bigger fish.

This fish is quite astonishing in other ways as well. It lives in a harem, one male and several females. Should the male disappear for any reason, one of the females will assume command of the group and take her duties so seriously that she will transform herself, several days later, into a fully functioning male.

Callionymidae

This small family with around fifteen species, each more beautiful than the next, ranges from tropical seas to the North Sea. This scaleless fish may be recognized by its elongated, nearly cylindrical body and its head, which is proportionally larger than its body. Two dorsal fins complement the highly developed ventral fins on which it likes to rest, for it lives on the sandy bottom, burrowing itself in as it searches for food.

Synchiropus splendidus

BLUE MANDARIN, DRAGONETTE

➤ *Philippines to eastern Australia* ➤ *Male: 4 in (10 cm); female: 2 1/3 in (6 cm)* ➤ *77°F (25°C)*
Males are very belligerent among themselves

It is regrettable that this scaleless fish, beautifully marbled with violet, green, and yellow markings, is so elusive. In the coral reefs that are its natural habitat, it anchors itself to the rocks on the sandy bottom. In the aquarium, it too often lives hidden from the eyes of its admiring owner. Adaptation in captivity is facilitated by providing it with ample space and many hiding places. Its diet is simple: crustaceans and algae. The Blue Mandarin is best kept alone, with only invertebrates as tankmates, so that there is little competition for food. Avoid placing two males together, or else they will have a fight to the finish.

Acanthuridae

This family of sprinters never lowers its guard–it is armed on either side of its caudal peduncle with a spine as formidable as a rapier. In the wild, tangs make use of these spines to intimidate other fish; in the aquarium, they often use them in fights to the death. Living in schools, they are aggressive toward their own species, but remain peaceful toward other fish. Since tangs greatly enjoy putting on sudden bursts of speed, a large aquarium is essential. They graze on algae and other plant matter. In the aquarium, they will accept live invertebrates.

Zebrasoma desjardinii

Sailfin Tang

➤ *Red Sea, western portion of the Indian Ocean, Mauritius*
➤ *12 to 16 in (31 to 41 cm)*
➤ *77° to 79°F (25° to 26°C)*
Can be aggressive

Although they are not great beauties, these fish have the advantage of being hardy and abundant. Thus, there is no feeding problem. For the *Z. desjardinii,* a fish that is sensitive to the weight of the years, its coloration will gradually fade. When young, it is easily acclimated, so purchasing adult specimens should be avoided. Once settled in, the Sailfin Tang alternates between animal and vegetable matter for its nourishment. Since it is rather aggressive toward other tangs, it is better to keep it alone. In the wild, it spreads out its large dorsal and anal fins to chase away intruders. Despite this acute territorial sense, it tolerates members of other families of fish.

Below:* Paracanthurus hepatus *(Blue Surgeonfish), from the same family as the Powder Blue Tang.

Acanthurus leucosternon

POWDER BLUE TANG

➤ *Indian and Pacific Oceans* ➤ *6 to 12 in (15 to 31 cm)* ➤ *79°F (26°C)*
Belligerent toward its family

As popular as its cousin the *Paracanthurus hepatus,* the Powder Blue Tang can be kept moderately successfully if its acclimation period is a success. Once acclimated, it must be kept in a large tank and generously fed with algae, other vegetable matter, and small crustaceans. Knowing that it eats slowly, you should spare it the company of overly voracious eaters. Two tangs cannot live together, since a battle to the death is practically inevitable. However, if you group several tangs together in a very large tank (at least 525 gal, 2,000 L), the balance of forces supports peace. Relations are good with species from other families.

Zebrasoma flavescens

Yellow Tang

➤ *Tropical Indian Ocean, Hawaiian Islands* ➤ *6 to 7 in (15 to 18 cm)*
➤ *77°F (25°C)*
Territorial

Except for its large, protruding black eye, this tang is yellow from snout to tail, including its fins. It hides a fearsome weapon–a sharp retractable spine–on either side of its caudal peduncle, which it uses to fiercely defend its territory. Any intruder will feel the sting of the Yellow Tang's spines. Nonetheless, the tang is aggressive only for a moment. Usually it is somewhat placid if the tank is large enough and provided with markers with which the tang can define the borders of its territory. In the wild its dietary regimen consists mostly of algae and small invertebrates. It adapts well to the aquarium when young and accepts all small prey.

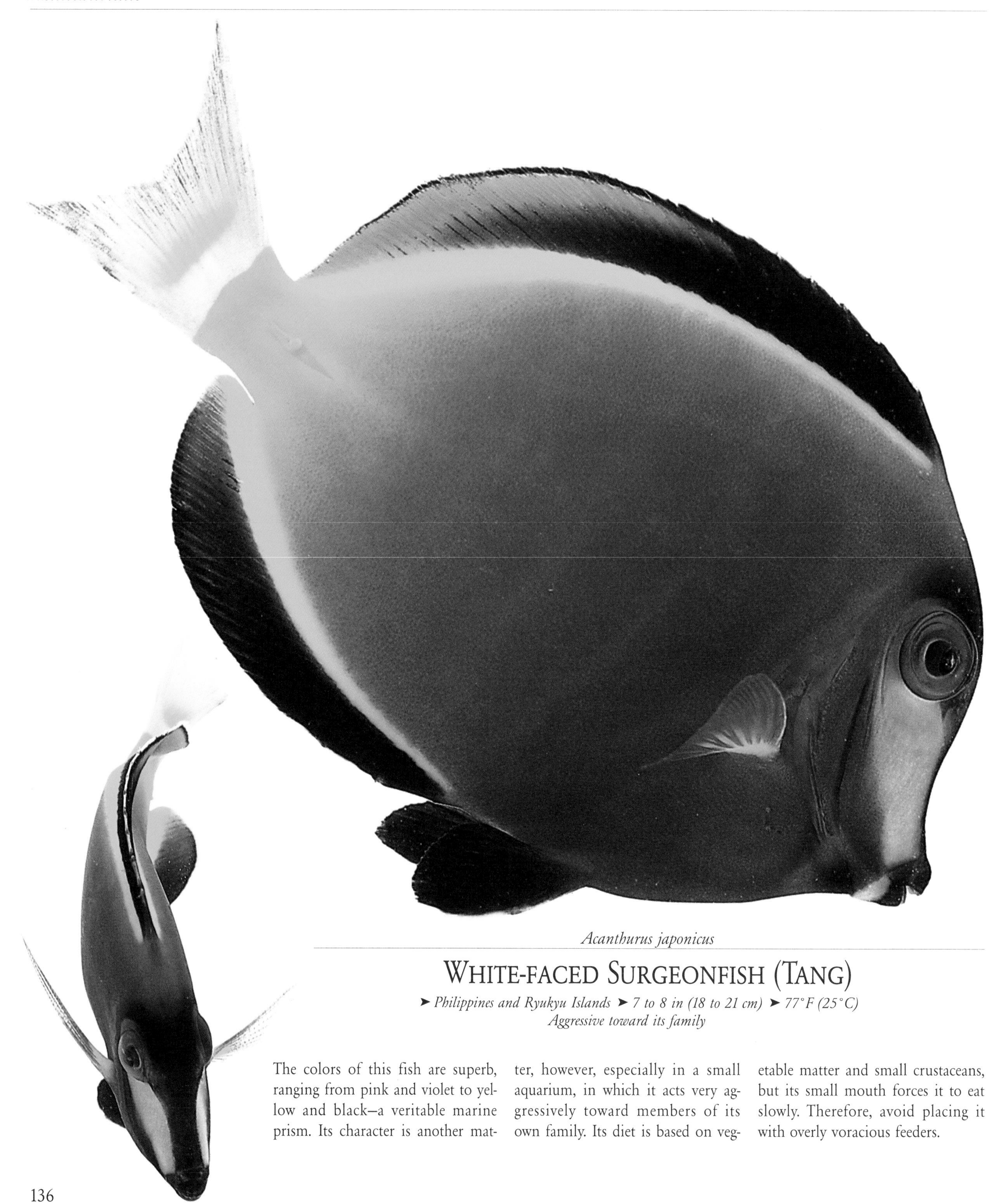

Acanthurus japonicus

White-faced Surgeonfish (Tang)

➤ *Philippines and Ryukyu Islands* ➤ *7 to 8 in (18 to 21 cm)* ➤ *77°F (25°C)*
Aggressive toward its family

The colors of this fish are superb, ranging from pink and violet to yellow and black–a veritable marine prism. Its character is another matter, however, especially in a small aquarium, in which it acts very aggressively toward members of its own family. Its diet is based on vegetable matter and small crustaceans, but its small mouth forces it to eat slowly. Therefore, avoid placing it with overly voracious feeders.

Naso lituratus

Naso Tang, Orange-spined Unicornfish

➤ Red Sea, Indo-Pacific region ➤ 8 to 12 in (21 to 31 cm) in the aquarium, up to 19 1/2 in (50 cm) in the wild ➤ 79°F (26°C)
Timid

After adaptation, which can be difficult, the Naso Tang is easily maintained. This timid fish is a big eater, and can therefore suffer from competition in feeding. Especially avoid placing it with voracious feeders, such as Black-spotted Puffers, who would soon deprive it of its meal. The sharp spines on either side of its caudal peduncle would not be of much help in such competition. Nonetheless, the owner of this fish should exercise caution when handling it or servicing the tank, for once its defense mechanism switches on, the fish can inflict a significant wound.

Left: The adult Naso Tang loses the white spots of its juvenile coat (below).

Siganidae

The Siganidae constitute a family of around thirty species. They are close relatives of the Surgeonfish, with whom they share the same habitat. Several species have emigrated from the Red Sea to establish themselves in the eastern Mediterranean. Others live in brackish water or even freshwater. They are called rabbitfish because of their short snout and continually twitching mouth. In addition, they are essentially herbivorous and live in groups. The analogy to rabbits ends there, for these attractive fish have hard rays on their fins that are hollowed out on each side with a groove filled with poisonous tissue. Although not fatal to humans, the sting of this fish is very painful and warrants medical treatment.

Siganus vulpinus

Foxface, Badgerface

➤ *Pacific Ocean* ➤ *6 to 10 in (15 to 26 cm)* ➤ *77°F (25°C)*
Hardy and peaceful

When at rest–the Foxface displays a splendid canary-yellow color. But when under stress, as in the photo above, the fish turns gray and marbled, so that the ocellus toward its posterior becomes blurred and the Foxface is no longer able to use it to trick potential adversaries. Although adaptation to the aquarium is not easy, it is nonetheless a hardy fish recommended for a first marine aquarium. The Foxface eats a little of everything. Feed it some small live prey and a good ration of vegetable matter. But do not attempt to handle this fish. Its fins contain a poison and can inflict a painful sting that, fortunately, is not deadly to fish hobbyists.

Balistidae

The hunting techniques of the Balistidae are unusual. Stationing themselves on the sandy bottom, these fish produce a strong current with their mouth, blowing away the sand and thereby bringing into view the prey concealed there. This family of twenty-six solitary and territorial species includes specimens that originate not only in tropical waters but also in the Atlantic Ocean and the Mediterranean Sea. (The French coast, for instance, is the home of Balistes capriscus.*) The body is covered with bony plates, and the eyes operate independently of each other. Moreover, these fish lack ventral fins. Instead they have three dorsal fins, each of which is equipped with a spine, which they brandish to frighten off intruders. They are called triggerfish because of their ability to lock the first dorsal spine in a vertical position by a very intricate mechanism. This technique enables them to seek shelter in rifts when resting at night and to resist strong currents.*

In the aquarium, the Balistidae adapt very well but should be placed only with large fish. They can survive longer than ten years.

Balistoides conspicillum

Clown Triggerfish

- *Indo-Pacific region*
- *12 to 19 1/2 in (31 to 50 cm)*
- *75° to 79°F (24° to 26°C)*

Tolerant of fish of the same size, except for those from its own family

The Clown Triggerfish is the perfect example of how beautiful saltwater fish can be. From its mouth, made up like that of a clown, to its numerous ocelli, which look like the photographic negative of a dalmatian one moment, and the next like the luminous pattern of a Provençal fabric, its sparkling colors leave no one unmoved. This large solitary creature is a poor choice for any who wish to make it the occupant of their first marine aquarium. It requires, in fact, the most spacious tank possible, one that is very well laid out and very well equipped, and occupied only by fish its own size. It enjoys a diet of all kinds of shellfish (both crustaceans and small mollusks), and it does not refuse invertebrates or even coral, which its powerful jaws, equipped with strong teeth, can easily crush. This fish is very expensive but relatively hardy and can live a long time.

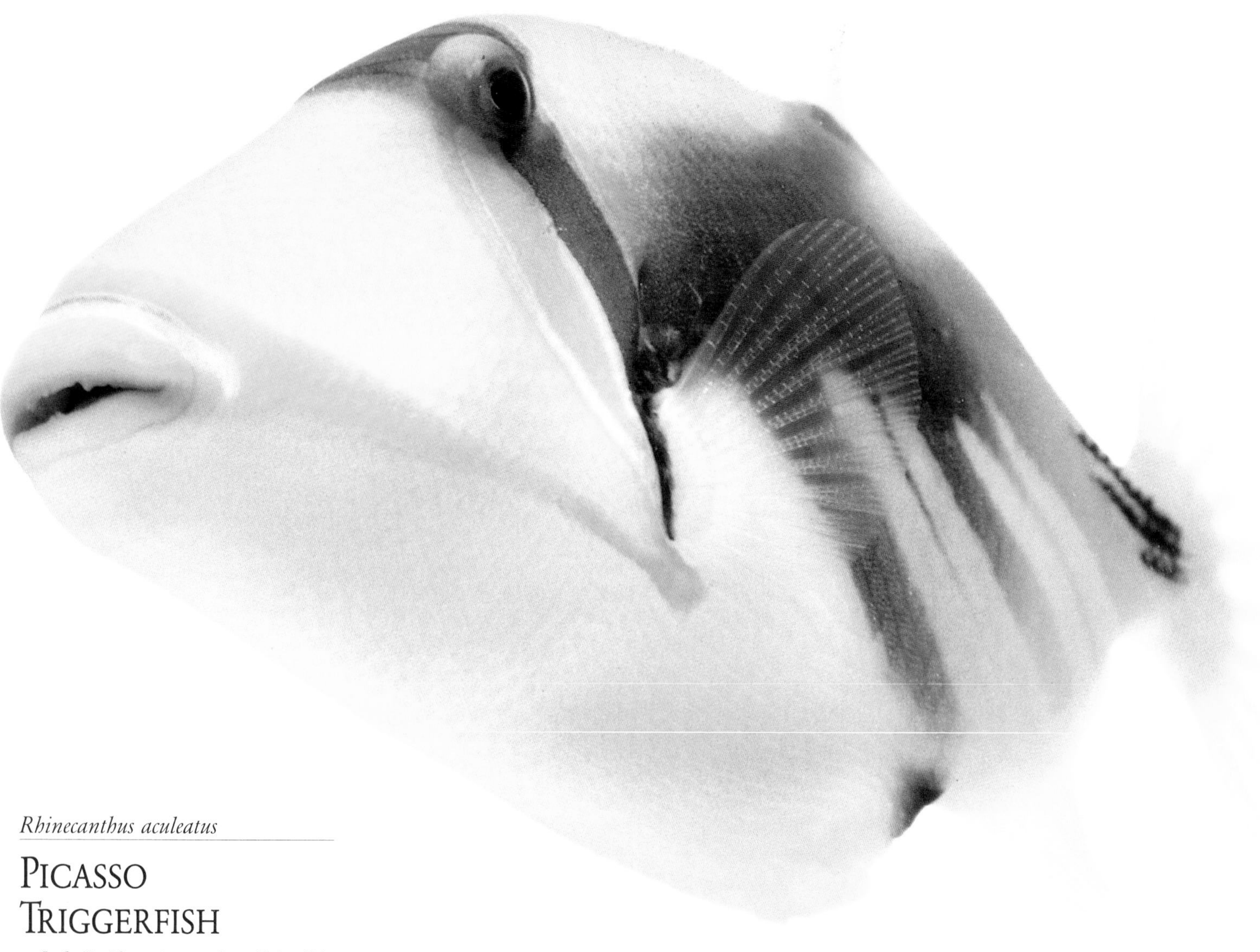

Rhinecanthus aculeatus

Picasso Triggerfish

➤ *Indo-Pacific region* ➤ *8 to 12 in (21 to 31 cm)* ➤ *77°F (25°C)*
Very territorial

The nonfigurative multicolored design of this fish inevitably makes one think of the canvases and drawings of the great master Picasso. It is more common than the Clown Triggerfish and noticeably less demanding as to the size of the aquarium, and its jaws like those of its cousin, are powerful crushing machines. This carnivore can eat anything: mussels, shrimp, fish, and sometimes pieces of lettuce, which assist its digestion. Pairing the fish is possible if they are chosen from the midst of a group of young fish. Otherwise, all efforts at placing Balistidae together end with the death of all but the most dominant fish.

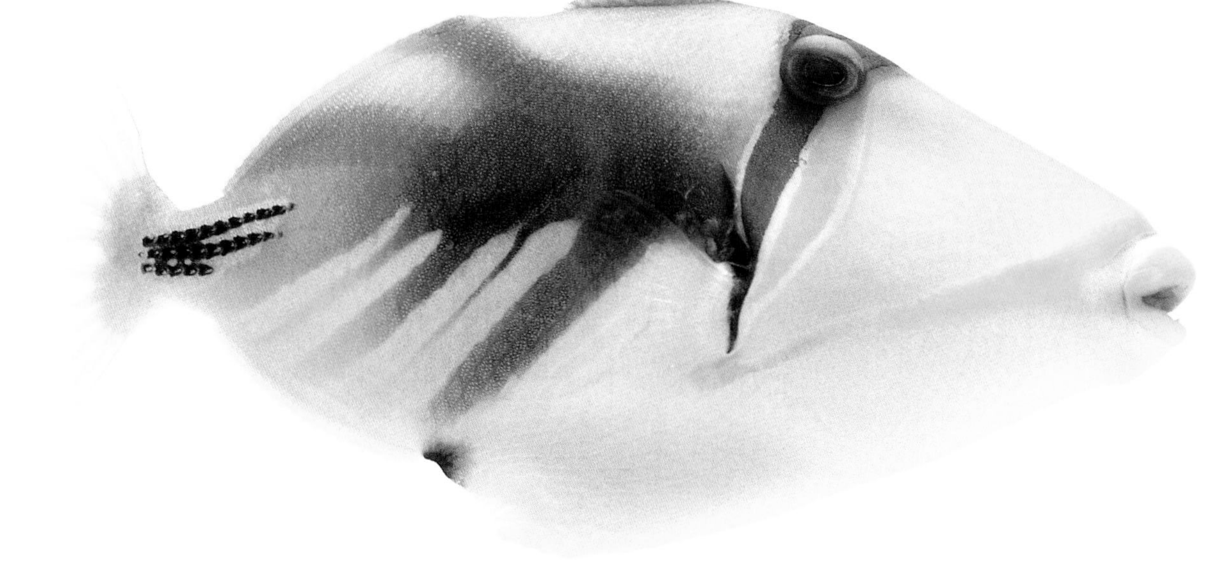

Ostraciidae

The shape of these fish is so odd that they are called boxfish. Comprising around thirty species, this family has some odd characteristics. Instead of scales, a carapace made up of hexagonal bony plates covers the head and body. Everything that is not carapace (the fins, eyes, and mouth) protrudes from openings in this protective shell. These fish are capable of maneuvering their eyes independently of each other, and instead of teeth, they are equipped with a dental plate, a fearsome tool that they operate only very slowly. They also are slow but skillful swimmers. In addition, as carriers of a highly toxic poison, they represent a fatal risk to the entire aquarium in the event of stress or death.

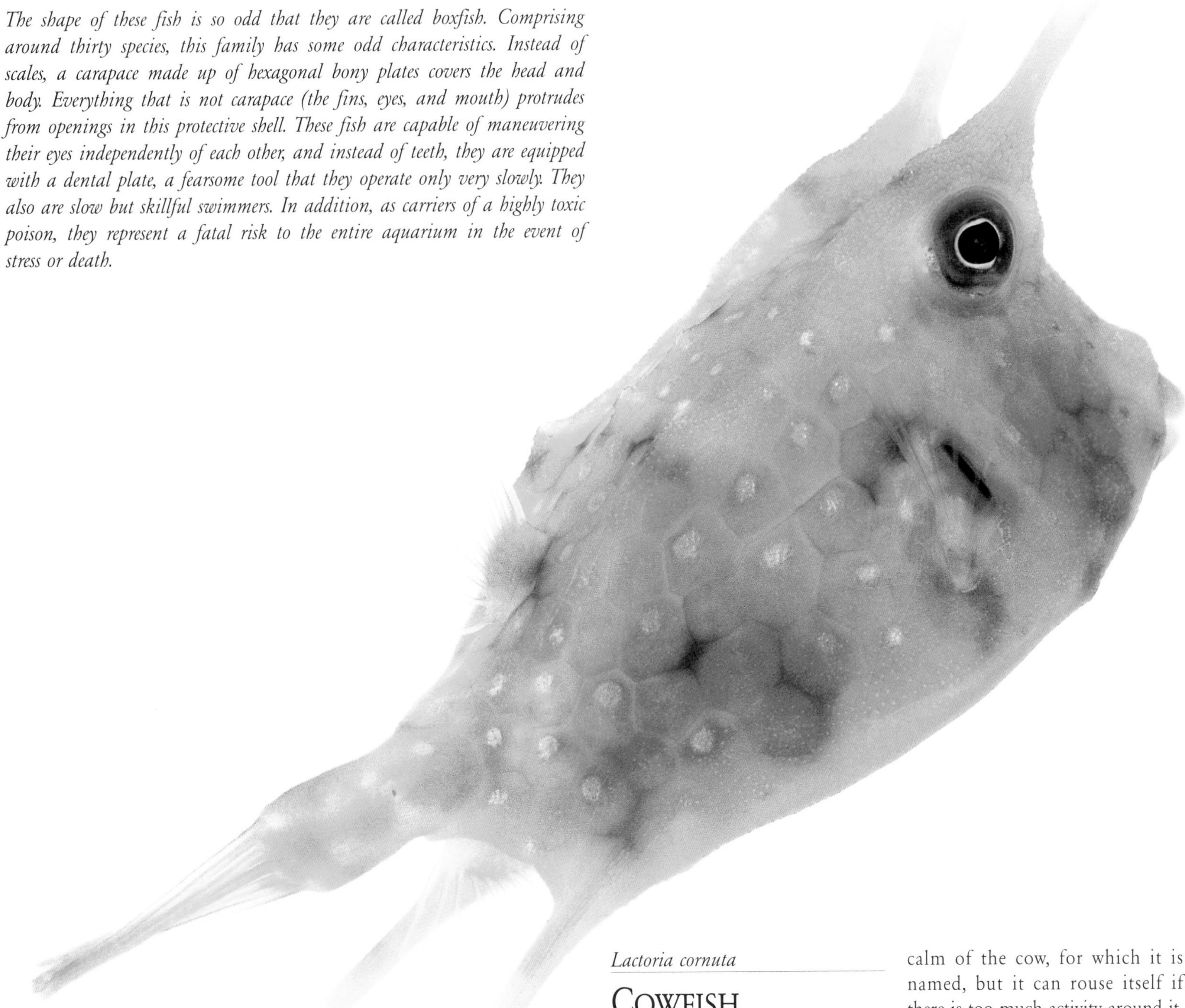

Lactoria cornuta

Cowfish, Longhorned Cowfish

➤ *Red Sea, Indo-Pacific region*
➤ *4 to 6 in (10 to 15 cm)*
➤ *77°F (25°C)*
Calm

This yellow, scaleless fish practices a stationary form of swimming. Equipped as it were with very weak fins, it moves about like a helicopter. It exhibits the imperturbable calm of the cow, for which it is named, but it can rouse itself if there is too much activity around it. Eating a little of everything and adapting easily, this unusual fish nonetheless presents one huge disadvantage: It is poisonous. At least this is the case when it dies and the poison that it carries can spread throughout the aquarium, first killing the microorganisms, then ever larger animals, raising the nitrite level in the tank. Any fish that has withstood the poison from the cowfish eventually succumbs to the increased nitrite level.

Index

common names

Index

scientific names

Photograph Credits

Except for the photographs listed here, all photographs were taken by Matthieu Prier

AQUA PRESS AGENCY:

p. 4 (1)
p. 10–11 (1)
p. 12–13 (3)
p. 14–15 (1)
p. 16–17 (1)
p. 18 (1)
p. 19 (1)
p. 20–21 (1)
p. 23 (1)
p. 24–25 (1)
p. 26–27 (2)
p. 29 (4)
p. 30–31 (1)
p. 32–33 (1)
p. 34–35 (1)
p. 43 (1) lower right
p. 45 (1) upper left
p. 46 (1) upper right
p. 48 (1) upper right
p. 49 (1) lower left
p. 50 (1) lower left
p. 52 (1) upper left
p. 66 (1) center left
p. 67 (1) upper left
p. 68 (1) center left
p. 108–109 (1)
p. 110 (1) lower left
p. 114 (1) lower right
p. 125 (1) below
p. 129 (1) lower left
p. 130 (1) upper left
p. 137 (1) above
p. 138 (1) below